C000160762

SYMBOLS KEY

The following symbols are used throughout this book:

@ address   ⊕ telephone   ⓦ website address   ⓔ email
🕒 opening times   Ⓝ public transport connections   ❶ important

The following symbols are used on the maps:

𝒊	information office	▪	points of interest
✈	airport	O	city
✚	hospital	O	large town
🛡	police station	○	small town
🚌	bus station	═	motorway
🚆	railway station	—	main road
Ⓜ	metro	—	minor road
✝	cathedral	—	railway
❶	numbers denote featured cafés & restaurants		

Hotels and restaurants are graded by approximate price as follows:
£ budget price   ££ mid-range price   £££ expensive

❶ Al- and El- simply mean "The" in Arabic and so are ignored in alphabetical listings in this guide, as well as in the index.

▶ View of Islamic Cairo

INTRODUCING
Cairo

Introduction

Cairo, or al-Qahira as it is known in Arabic, means 'The Triumphant', a fitting name for a city that not only survives but positively thrives in the face of challenges.

The capital city of Egypt stretches along 40 km (25 miles) of the River Nile and has a population estimated at around 18 million, although no one is certain of the actual number. Cairo is the largest and most populated capital in Africa, a long-time cultural hub of the Middle East and a major player in the Mediterranean community.

A geographical and cultural nexus, the city is a lively mix of dramatic contrasts that encompasses the wonders of Oriental bazaars, the brash pizzazz of 21st-century shopping centres and the very present realities of pollution, noise and sheer volume of people. But as much as Cairo can be hard work, it also offers some spectacularly satisfying rewards. This is a city of old-world charm and adventure. Visitors typically come to experience such well-known attractions as the pyramids and the enigmatic beauty of the treasures in the Egyptian Museum. When they arrive, however, they find so much more to savour, including its skyline of graceful domes and towering, sculpted minarets that casts a spell over everyday city life, the solemn majesty of Coptic churches and the buzz of open-air cafés. Indeed, Cairo is known for its beating heart, the frenetic vivacity of its streets and the outgoing generosity of its people.

Complementing the manifold major attractions are spontaneous vignettes, such as the sight of the banks of the Nile littered with young couples engrossed in the sounds of the latest Arabic pop sensations. On a visit to the capital you will find not only the Cairo of story books, which still exists today beneath just a few layers of dust, but also a constantly evolving, incessantly appealing 21st-century city.

◆ *Historic treasures in the Egyptian Museum*

When to go

Cairo will captivate you all year long and, unless you're likely to be put off by the sometimes sweltering summer heat (see below), any time is a great time to visit. When planning your trip, though, you will want to bear in mind that during the religious observance of Ramadan (see page 10) schedules will change, sites will have reduced hours and your daytime refuelling options will be reduced. Restaurant reservations at this time are a must and many eateries operate on set menus that are pricier than normal. The only places in which you will legally be able to buy alcohol during this month are hotels. Despite those limitations, for some travellers experiencing Ramadan is a special treat, to see first-hand how the holy month is celebrated in the liveliest Muslim city in the world.

SEASONS & CLIMATE

Cairo enjoys almost year-round sunshine. While the winter months between December and February see some cloud and rain, temperatures rarely drop below 10°C (50°F). In March and April, strong, hot winds (known to Europeans as the sirocco and to Egyptians as the *khamsin*) blow in from the desert, sometimes with such intensity that the city finds itself in the middle of a sandstorm. In summer months, most Cairenes escape the intense heat that regularly hits between 35°C and 40°C (95–104°F) for nearby beaches on the Mediterranean and Red Sea coasts. Spring and autumn are probably the best times to enjoy Cairo, with friendlier temperatures around 25°C (77°F) and unending sunshine.

ANNUAL EVENTS

January
Cairo International Book Fair is one of the biggest in the world, with over 3,000 exhibitors and three million visitors per year. The event is a cultural landmark, attracting intellectuals, publishers, writers and bibliophiles. Ⓦ www.egyptianbook.org.eg

February
Al Nitaq Festival Held in a variety of venues throughout the city, Al Nitaq is a popular, month-long festival of poetry, music and other outpourings of creativity.

March
Sham an-Naseem The celebration of the coming of spring dates from the time of the Pharaohs. It's the Egyptian equivalent of Easter, and children busy themselves painting eggs. Families picnic outdoors and lunch on salted fish.

April & May
Moulids These spring celebrations are lively parties and processions in which people take to the streets of Cairo on the birthdays of various saints (see page 12).

August
Wafaa el-Nil Festival, meaning 'Fidelity of the Nile Festival', is a contemporary event echoing the ancient Egyptian veneration of the river. There are art competitions for children, poetry readings, concerts and scientific discussions held all over the city.

○ *Team riders in The Pharaoh's Rally*

September
Rallye des Pharaons is a week-long international endurance race of 3,000 km (1,865 miles) that winds its way through the Sahara desert. The event begins at the feet of the Sphinx in Giza and concludes in Cairo. Ⓦ www.rallyedespharaons.it

Ramadan The holy period is the ninth month of the Islamic lunar calendar. Days are quiet and many shops close early so owners can make it home before sunset, when they break fast with their families. Evenings are festive, and cafés and restaurants are packed until sunrise, when the fast begins again.

November & December
The Cairo International Film Festival This cinefest for cinephiles
has been drawing crowds since its inception in 1976.
Ⓦ www.cairofilmfest.org

PUBLIC HOLIDAYS
Secular holidays
Police Day 25 Jan
Sinai Liberation 25 Apr
Labour Day 1 May
Evacuation Day 18 June
Bank Holiday 1 July
Revolution Anniversary 23 July
Armed Forces Day 6 Oct

Religious holidays
Eastern Orthodox Christmas 7 Jan
Moulid el-Nabi (Prophet's Birthday) 15 Feb 2011, 4 Feb 2012,
24 Jan 2013
Sham el-Nessim (Eastern Orthodox Easter) 24 Apr 2011,
15 Apr 2012, 5 May 2013
Ramadan Commences 11 Aug 2010, 1 Aug 2011, 20 July 2012
Eid ul-Fitr (End of Ramadan) 10 Sept 2010, 30 Aug 2011,
19 Aug 2012
Eid ul-Adha 16 Nov 2010, 6 Nov 2011, 26 Oct 2012
Muharram (Islamic New Year) 7 Dec 2010, 26 Nov 2011,
15 Nov 2012

Moulids

For Egyptians – Muslim and Christian alike – the word *moulid*, which technically refers to a celebration of the birthdays of revered saints, conjures up images of carnival lights, dancing through the night and mass indulgence in sticky sweets.

Islamic *moulids* are based on the lunar calendar, and thus take a bit of pre-planning as dates shift back by 11 days each year. Although these celebrations are not a strictly Orthodox practice, they're a popular tradition of Muslim life in Egypt, particularly among the less privileged sections of society. Nobody knows when they began, although it is established that they were celebrated in the Fatimid and Ayyubid periods (see page 14) by government officials and spiritual leaders. They are equivalent in many ways to the celebrations of Jesus' birthday, and some believe that the festivities arose during the Crusades, when Islamic and Christian cultures influenced each other.

More of an Islamic custom than a religious observance, then, *moulids* are family occasions where people come together for food, sweets (*Halawet el-moulid*, confectionery specially made for the occasion) and the enjoyment of one another's company. They vary in duration but all reach a climax with the *Leila el-Kebira*, or 'Big Night'. This occasion is the time for men to don their traditional *galabiyas* (long gowns) and perform the *Zikr*, a ritual Sufi dance where they sway back and forth and move their bodies to drum and tambourine music while a singer performs devotional chants.

An evening of a *moulid* is filled with music and song emanating from the different tents that are packed together into the small streets and squares. The place for the country's largest and most colourful processions is Midan Al-Hussein in Islamic Cairo. As you walk from tent to tent, stop to taste the sweets and chat with the many Egyptians who will want to explain their traditions to you.

If you are lucky enough to be in Cairo during any of the annual *moulids*, be prepared for extreme crowds, blaring music and a very good time. Like much else here, they are stimulating, exhausting and well worth experiencing.

● *A busy alley during* moulid *celebrations*

History

Although Cairo is Egypt's capital today, its central position in the country's story is a relatively recent development – in fact, it did not even exist when the pyramids at Giza were constructed in Memphis, around 24 km (15 miles) south of present-day Cairo's main square. By the time the urban entity that we recognise today as Cairo began to coalesce, those astonishing monuments to dead pharaohs were already ancient history.

Today's city occupies land that was once the site of smaller ancient settlements which became increasingly prominent during Roman times. The Romans realised that, due to its location at the nexus of the Red Sea and the Nile, Babylon-on-the-Nile (as it was called), a site that's now part of today's Old Cairo district, would have tremendous strategic importance. In 640, a Muslim army commander, Amr Ibn al-As, managed to conquer the 'Fortress of Babylon' and subsequently introduced Islam to the country. He founded a settlement called Al-Fustat on the East bank of the Nile and built Africa's first mosque. Al-Fustat was the major centre of power in Egypt for over three centuries, until the Fatimids invaded the region in 969 and established a new city, Al-Qahira, just north of Al-Fustat. In 1168, Al-Fustat was destroyed by its own rulers to prevent Crusaders from capturing it, and the administrative capital of Egypt moved permanently to Al-Qahira, the site of what is today's central Cairo.

For several centuries, power shifted between the Ayyubids, the Mamelukes, the Ottomans and the French under Napoleon. The latter's expulsion resulted in the installation of Muhammad Ali, who is regarded as the founder of modern Egypt.

The birth of modern Cairo came in the 1860s, when the ruler Ismail, Mohammed Ali's grandson, expanded the city along the Nile, employing European architects and planners to design a conurbation in the style of the Continent's great boulevard-based cities. The Suez Canal was completed in 1869. It wasn't long before Europe came to Egypt once again, this time in the form of the British, who purchased Egypt's share of the canal and, in 1882, became the final foreign rulers of the country. Although Egypt gained its independence in 1922, the British remained until 1956.

Soon after the completion of the Suez Canal, Cairo attracted the attention of the whole world and tourism and business boomed. The revolution of 1952, also known as the July 23 Revolution, brought the monarchy to an end with a bloodless military coup, as Muhammad Naguib and Gamal Abdel Nasser became the first and second Egyptians to rule over an Egypt republic. Nasser is credited with furthering the cause of pan-Arab nationalism. Anwar Al Sadat came to power in 1970 after Nasser's death. Although he helped lead the October War against Israel in 1973, also known as the Yom Kippur War, he was eventually awarded the Nobel Peace Prize for his efforts in achieving the 1979 Egypt–Israel Peace Treaty. He was assassinated in Cairo in 1981 during a high-profile victory parade.

Hosni Mubarek has been in power ever since, presiding over sometimes challenging times. Increased foreign investment and economic reforms over the last half-century have exacerbated the gap between the country's haves and have-nots, and in recent years the country's Muslim Brotherhood, a Sunni movement, has gained mainstream popularity. Despite Egypt's political and religious ups and downs, however, its capital Cairo has always remained a fascinating, historic, place to visit.

Lifestyle

Malish just might be the word you will hear most in Cairo.
It means 'no problem', and Cairenes are characterised by the
spirit of perseverance that shines out through their friendly
smiles and laid back attitude. The virtues of the uncomplicated
life are celebrated here. Simple *ahwas* (traditional coffee houses)
are filled with patrons sucking on their bubbling shisha pipes,
reading newspapers and playing backgammon.

Other phrases you'll hear are *Insha-Allah* ('God willing'),
Alhamdullillah ('all thanks to God') and any number of other

ISLAM'S FIVE BASIC PILLARS

There are five formal acts of worship that Muslims believe
strengthen their faith.

Testimony of faith (*Kalima*) The cornerstone of the Muslim
faith is the profession 'There is no god but God;
Muhammad is the prophet of Allah'.

Prayer (*Salat*) There are five compulsory daily prayers that
remind Muslims of God.

Almsgiving (*Zakat*) Those who can afford to pay alms give
two-and-a-half per cent of their wealth to the needy.

Fasting (*Sawm*) This is the month-long fast of Ramadan,
during which Muslims abstain from eating and drinking
from sunrise to sundown.

Pilgrimage (*Hajj*) Pilgrimage is made to Mecca in Saudi
Arabia at least once in a Muslim's lifetime.

🔺 *Relaxing in Al-Azhar Park with a view of the city*

references to God's powers and providence. In fact, the last decade has witnessed a rise in overt religiosity, with an increasing number of Muslim women wearing the veil and religious rhetoric playing a major role in the country's discourse. Cairo is famous for its *muezzins*, the men whose calls to prayer echo from minarets five times each day. The practical demands of faith affect the lifestyle here, and you will see shops closing up while their owners pray. It's not uncommon to witness people praying in the street.

Mosques play a key part in daily life. The major ones are always open (only the mosques that deviate from that rule of thumb have their opening hours listed in this guide) and almost always accept visitors. Do avoid going inside them during the Friday midday prayer, as this is a busy time and there is limited space.

In Cairo, family is still paramount and is a buffer against the stresses of modern life. Even among strangers, though, there is a camaraderie that is unique to the free-spirited and quick-witted Egyptians.

Culture

Cairo is a place where different civilisations have been crossing paths for centuries, and this has left its distinctive mark on the city. The blend of influences and diverse outlooks is a part of the natural history of Cairo and is encountered on every street corner. Add to this a lively arts scene that's currently experiencing a surge of energy from younger generations, and you can start to understand why Cairo is the exciting cultural hub of the entire wider region.

The city boasts a film industry that's prolific and creative enough to merit its nickname, 'the Hollywood of the Middle East', and Arabs around the world recognise Cairo's streets in such movies as the classic *The Yacoubian Building*. This tells the story of the inhabitants of a downtown Cairo apartment building and lifts the lid on the less savoury aspects of city life, including prostitution, corruption and a highly stratified class system. Both the film and the book it was based on gained deserved international attention and will hopefully help the film industry continue its work, not only in the comedy and romance genres that it mastered long ago, but in more serious cinema.

Cairo possesses the world's liveliest belly dancing scene. You can choose from a variety of venues in which to get your fill of the shimmy, ranging from evening Nile cruise rides with live bands and dance performances to the stretch of bawdy and boisterous nightclubs on the road to the pyramids.

There is a lively music scene that's broad enough to satisfy most tastes, and visitors can choose anything from classical

◯ *Belly dancing is a popular entertainment in Cairo*

European orchestral performances to the native instrument ensembles of Oriental music. The pop scene is flourishing, especially among the younger generations. Innovative sounds emanate from bands such as Wust al-Balad (which means 'Downtown') and Eskenderella who play to captivated audiences across the city in favourite night spots such as **After Eight** (ⓐ 6 Sharia Qasr el-Nil, Downtown ❶ (02) 339 8000 ◷ 20.00–03.00 Sun–Wed, 20.00–04.00 Thur–Sat) and **Cairo Jazz Club** (ⓐ 197 Sharia 26th of July, Agouza ❶ (03) 345 9939 ◷ 19.00–03.00) or more family-oriented complexes like El Sawy Culture Wheel (see page 63).

There are scores of cultural centres and outdoor stages to enjoy in Cairo. As a visitor, you can take advantage of the performances put on in hotels and restaurants, or you can dive further into Egyptian life by peering into venues like the **Ganeena Theatre** in Al-Azhar Park (ⓐ Sharia Salah Salem ❶ (02) 510 3868 ⓦ www.alazharpark.com) where evening musical performances enchant audiences in a spectacular setting that overlooks the 12th-century Ayyubid old city wall.

For listings of cultural events in Cairo, ask at the tourist office (see page 134) or check the publications recommended on page 31. Note that last-minute changes to events and times are common, so if you're making a special trip to a venue it's a good idea to call ahead rather than rely on second-hand information.

◗ *Night view of the Nile from Cairo Tower*

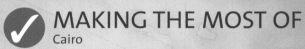

MAKING THE MOST OF
Cairo

Shopping

There are several retail options here, from gift shops selling handmade crafts to bustling local souqs (markets or bazaars) and air-conditioned malls. For souvenirs, most people head to Khan al-Khalili, running parallel to Al-Azhar Street. This is one of the world's oldest bazaars and is also a tourist magnet, so the tackiness factor is considerable. That said, with a bit of patience you can find spectacular buys.

Head west for a more authentic souq experience. For fabrics (including Egyptian cotton) try the Wekalet al-Balah (Tent Makers' Bazaar), which lies between Al-Azhar Mosque (see page 71) and the Citadel (see page 74). This bazaar is great

BARGAINING TIPS

Bargaining requires certain skills. Do your research and come prepared with data on the price-profile of the desired products. Other things to remember:

- Before you start, convert the asking price into your home currency to see if haggling will be worthwhile.
- Feel free to accept tea from the shopkeeper. It doesn't obligate you to buy and it's a nice way to socialise.
- Always be polite and have a sense of humour – it's supposed to be fun!
- If the asking price is unreasonable, walking away from a stall is usually a sure way to get the price to fall.

USEFUL SHOPPING PHRASES

What time do the shops open/close?
Il mahal hayiftah/biyi'fil isa'a kam?

How much is this?
Bee kam da?

Can I try this on?
Mumkan agarab da?

My size is...
Ma-asi...

Do you have change?
Ma'ak/i fakka?

I'd like to buy...
'Ayz/a ashtiree...

I'll take it
Hakhud da

This is too large/too small. Do you have any others?
Da kibeer/sagheer awy. Fee aya hagga tani?

for appliqué-work, while Sharia Mohammed Ali is notable for musical instruments.

Note that many owner-run shops and other small venues either don't have phones or don't often answer them! Opening hours can also vary depending on the season or how busy it is. If you're dead set on entering a particular shop and arrive to find it closed, ask around as the owner may be somewhere in the vicinity.

Eating & drinking

From *mezzeh* and salad spreads to delicately grilled meats and fresh seafood, you'll find Egyptian food hearty and delicious. The mass of options includes nibbles bought from food carts on side streets (typically, baked sweet potatoes and barbecued corn) and the fine fare produced during the extravagant 'food weeks' that are regularly organised at deluxe hotels. The other good news is that most of the food here comes at a pleasantly reasonable price.

Traditional Egyptian fare is a real treat. *Fuul* (mashed beans) and *taameya* (fried bean patties) are commonly eaten for breakfast and are readily available from street vendors – ask your hotel concierge to recommend a hygienic one in your neighbourhood, or hit Downtown, where the popular **FelFela** (ⓐ 15 Sharia Hoda Shaarawy ⓣ (02) 392 2833 ⓛ 08.00–23.00 ⓜ Metro: Sadat) has both a sit-down restaurant and stand-up takeaway.

Koshary can be said to be Egypt's national dish. Eaten at any time of the day, this mix of macaroni, lentils, chick peas, rice, fried onion and tomato sauce can also be dressed with *shutta* (chilli sauce). Cairenes flock to the legendary **Koshary Abu Tarek** (ⓐ 16 Sharia Champollion, Downtown ⓣ (02) 577 5935 ⓜ Metro:

PRICE CATEGORIES
Ratings are based on the approximate cost of a three-course meal for one person, excluding drinks.
£ up to 40LE   ££ 40–80LE   £££ over 80LE

USEFUL DINING PHRASES

I would like a table for... people, please
'Ayz/a tarabiiza li... shukhs, lau samaht/i

May I see the menu, please?
Mumkin el-menu, lau samaht/i

Where is the toilet, please?
Fen il hammaam, lau samaht/i

I am a vegetarian. Does this dish contain meat?
Ana nabaty/ya. Fey lahma fel akla dey?

May I have the bill, please?
Mumkin il hasab, lau samaht/i

I would like a cup of coffee/tea
'Ayz/a ahwa/shay

Sadat) to stock up on real-deal *koshary*, and there's no reason why you shouldn't join them.

Visitors who at home customarily round off a night out with anything resembling a 'kebab' will be shocked to find their *shawarma* sandwich served on a white bun. Make sure that if you are hankering for the flat-bread version you specify *'aish shami'*, which means Syrian bread.

The other must-have is *fiteer*. These pastries can be served either sweet or savoury, and while the latter do bear a resemblance to pizzas, the sweet ones, served with anything from icing sugar to chocolate spread, are really more of a dessert. You'll find *fiteer* in pastry shops and cafés all over the city. Oriental desserts will sweeten your stay, so be sure to sample more than just the *baklava* (or *ba'lawa*, as Egyptians call it), and give other syrupy treats like *basbousa*, *kounefa* and *lomital ady* a try. These local

● *The Revolving Restaurant at the Grand Hyatt Cairo (see page 39)*

DRINKING IN CAIRO

Cairo is known for its drinks possibilities. You can head to bars for the booze or enjoy the city's more popular drinking experience in the *ahwas*, where beverages range from fresh strawberry juice in the summer to a hot, milky cinnamon drink in the winter. The fresh juices will blow you away and are guaranteed to give you a hankering for Cairo well after your visit is over.

treats are potently sweet variations of cheese-and-nut fillings in semolina and filo pastry shells. Another delight, *sahleb*, is a sweet, milky concoction with nuts and raisins. It can be served either as a drink, or thick like a dessert, to be eaten with a spoon.

The most popular way to while away the time is at the traditional *ahwa*, a sort of coffee shop that offers considerably more than coffee. These are everywhere and well worth a visit. A popular spot for inexpensive drinks and shisha is downtown in the Bustan, an alley behind Café Riche (see page 65) on Talaat Harb. Many eateries in Cairo are also clubs that provide live and/or recorded music, so a nibble and a boogie will often be on the menu.

A rather annoying phenomenon introduced by restaurateurs is a minimum amount you have to spend; it amounts to an entry fee. Oddly, many menus are not being changed to reflect this, which means that you are simply forced to buy more food, or at least pay for it. Price categories in this guide reflect applicable minimum charges.

Entertainment & nightlife

Egyptians know how to have a party, and how to keep the fun going all night long. So you'll have a good time here, and there are lots of options catering to many different tastes. Wednesdays and Thursdays are the big nights out. As the sun goes down, the people come out and the serious business of eating, drinking, dancing and making merry goes on into the wee small hours, with most places staying open until around 3 or 4 am. Still others are 24-hour hedonist haunts, only calming down long after the morning prayer has been called; it's then that you will appreciate the damage that the *muezzin*'s cry can inflict on a severely dehydrated central nervous system.

Since Egypt is a Muslim country, many Cairenes enjoy themselves on soft drinks, though alcohol is not difficult to come by for those who want it (and you will find it easy to link up with a crowd, Muslims most definitely included, with whom you can gel).

The most basic and popular night out for the locals will be spent at *baladi* bars. Often called 'cafeterias' to disguise the fact that they serve alcohol, they are perfectly safe, though a little boisterous, and women on their own might feel uncomfortable in what is essentially a male domain. If you want to seek some out, try the Alfy Street area around Midan Orabi.

Things swing in a decidedly upmarket direction, too. The arrival on the nightlife scene of the super-elite **Buddha Bar** at the Sofitel al-Gezira (ⓐ 3 Sharia al-Thawra Council, Zamalek ⓣ (02) 737 3737 ⓜ Metro: Gezira) must surely get the trend-

● *Catch a whirling dervish performance*

setters' seal of approval. If you are willing to pay a comparatively large sum of money for your evening here, you will enjoy the view of both the Nile and of Cairo's hip, moneyed crowd. If you don't want to spend too much, all the main hotels have Western-style bars where Cairenes and foreigners congregate for an ice-melting drink.

🔺 *Enjoy a relaxing night out at one of the many international hotel bars*

If you're after a nightclub, call it a disco and head for the hotel chains, or check out any of the many venues that the young, well-to-do locals frequent. After Eight (see page 68) puts on a packed Thursday night party, with live bands swapping seamlessly between Top 40 hits and Arabic pop favourites to the delight of the expats and Egyptians who fill the dance floor, desperate for an opportunity to display their dancing prowess. Also be sure to see what's playing at the Cairo Jazz Club (see page 68), which offers a sophisticated mix of live jazz, blues and a DJ. **Africana** (● Pyramids Road, Giza) is something very different again, namely a noisy, crowded and energetic venue with a sub-Saharan vibe.

Many nightclubs require reservations, so try to call ahead to make sure you get in. Going out means looking good in Cairo, so dress smart: it might be your sartorial ticket to a truly memorable night.

WHAT'S ON?

There are several monthly listings magazines to choose from. *G Magazine* and *iCroc* (Ⓦ www.icroc.com) can be found in American-style coffee shops, bookstores and some restaurants. Also check Ⓦ www.yallabina.com, as well as *Al-Ahram Weekly* (Ⓦ http://weekly.ahram.org.eg), or the monthly *Egypt Today* (Ⓦ www.egypttoday.com). Even when you've consulted one of the above, you might want to call ahead to confirm the listings as timings and events can change right up to the last minute.

Sport & relaxation

City life makes exercise and relaxation much sought-after commodities. One of Cairo's most attractive parks is the lovely Al-Azhar Park on Sharia Salah Salem. This is where you can breathe the city's cleanest air.

SPECTATOR SPORTS

Cairo is a major football town, with local rivalry concentrating on two teams, **Al-Ahly Club** (Ⓦ www.ahly.com) and **Zamalek** (Ⓦ www.zamalek-sc.com). The highly regarded national team has had continuing success in international tournaments and plies its silky skills on the turf of the National Stadium.
Cairo National Stadium ⓐ Sharia Youssef Abbas & Salah Salem, Nasr City

PARTICIPATION SPORTS

Belly dancing In Egypt this is an art form and a sport (just ask your abdominals once you've had a go). A crash course in the ancient dance is fun. **Madame Raqia Hassan** (Ⓣ (02) 748 2338 Ⓦ www.raqiahassan.net), instructor to some of the country's top dancers, runs private lessons for beginners. The London-based **Raqs Sharqi Society** (Ⓣ www.raqssharqisociety.org) will be able to put you in touch with other teachers and schools in Cairo.

Golf It's the same the whole world over, you might think – but not many courses can compete with Mena House's view of the pyramids.

Hotel Oberoi Mena House ⓐ Pyramids Road, Giza ⓣ (03) 377 3222 or 376 6644 ⓛ 07.00–sunset

Horse riding Mounting a trusty steed will offer you great exercise and fabulous views of the pyramids. Do choose your stable carefully, though, as many of the horses in Egypt are, unfortunately, poorly tended. The best local establishments are in Nazlet as-Samaan, and are called **MG** (ⓣ (02) 358 3832) and **AA** (ⓣ (02) 385 0531).

RELAXATION

Spas There is a superb selection of spas in Cairo, especially in its luxury hotels. Two excellent outfits are **La Rose Spa** (ⓐ 58 Sharia Gezirat al-Arab, Mohandiseen ⓣ (03) 302 8577 ⓦ www.larosespa.com ⓛ 10.00–21.00), which provides services from Moroccan baths to manicures, and **Mohamed al Sagheer** (ⓐ 16 Sharia Salah al-Din, Zamalek ⓣ (02) 736 3501 ⓛ 10.00–22.00), from whose pampering clutches you may never want to wriggle free.

▲ *Golf with a view of the pyramids*

Accommodation

In Cairo you will find plenty of options in every price bracket. Perhaps the best way to narrow down your choices to a manageable range is to decide if you would like a hotel near the pyramids, near the airport (at Heliopolis, see page 48), in the centre of town or in some of the quieter neighbourhoods such as Zamalek. Rates tend to fluctuate by season, increasing between April and October. Public and religious holidays are also busy times. Hotels for those on a budget can mostly be found in central Cairo, between Midan Tahrir and the train station. Wherever you choose, it's wisest to make your reservations early. You should also consider the weather when booking accommodation – if visiting in the heat of summer, it's definitely worth paying extra for air-conditioning.

HOTELS

Berlin Hotel £ Well located in central Downtown, this hotel is close to Talaat Harb and Qasr el-Nil, with their intriguing backstreets, *ahwas* and *shawarmas*. ➋ 2 Sharia Shawarby, Downtown (Central Cairo) ➊ (02) 395 7502 ➌ berlinhotelcairo@hotmail.com ➍ Metro: Sadat

PRICE CATEGORIES

Accommodation ratings in this book are based on the average price of a room for two people between April and October, including breakfast, unless otherwise stated.

£ up to 150LE   ££ 150–500LE   £££ over 500LE

⬥ *The Cairo Marriott Hotel is one of the largest in the Middle East*

Garden City House Hotel £ A comfortable favourite. Balcony views of the Nile beat the noise of other Downtown budget stops hands down. ⓐ 23 Sharia Kamal al-Din Salah, Garden City (Central Cairo) ⓣ (02) 794 8400 or 794 4969 ⓦ www.gardencityhouse.com ⓜ Metro: Sadat

Al-Hussein Hotel £ If you want to be in the centre of Islamic Cairo and don't mind the din, this is the place for you. While rooms are very simple and faded, you'll enjoy the rooftop view of the minarets in the Khan al-Khalili. ⓐ Midan Hussein, Khan al-Khalili (Islamic Cairo) ⓣ (02) 591 8089

Lotus Hotel £ A long-time favourite due to the friendly staff, convenient location and value. ⓐ 12 Sharia Talaat Harb, Downtown (Central Cairo) ⓣ (02) 575 0966 ⓦ www.lotushotel.com ⓜ Metro: Sadat

Golden Tulip Hotel Flamenco Cairo ££ In the affluent neighbourhood of Zamalek, the Tulip is located beside a small shopping arcade that has a grocer's, a dry cleaner's and many other conveniences. Rooms are clean and simple, and there's a fitness centre, spa and in-room air-conditioning and TV. ⓐ 2 Sharia al Geziret al-Wusta, Zamalek (Central Cairo) ⓣ (02) 735 0815 ⓦ www.flamencohotels.com

Mayfair Hotel ££ The staff are personable and helpful, rooms clean and prices reasonable. A peaceful atmosphere in a quiet neighbourhood. Free Wi-Fi. ⓐ 9 Aziz Osman, Zamalek (Central Cairo) ⓣ (02) 735 7315 ⓦ www.mayfaircairo.com

President Hotel ££ Situated in Zamalek on a hip street, with a number of fashionable restaurants in the vicinity. The gourmet restaurant on the 11th floor has an excellent view. ⓐ 22 Sharia Taha Hussein, Zamalek (Central Cairo) ⓣ (02) 735 0718 ⓦ www.presidenthotelcairo.com

Talisman Hotel ££ Cairo's leading boutique hotel. The Talisman's individually decorated rooms and exquisite common areas equal superb value. You will experience excellent service and have handy free access to a computer with internet. Although you'll have to struggle on without the amenities of luxury hotels, you will be very comfortable here. Reservations are a must. ⓐ 39 Sharia Talaat Harb (Central Cairo) ⓣ (02) 393 9431 ⓦ http://talisman-hotel.com

Windsor Hotel ££ Once a royal bathhouse, then a British Officers' Club, this is conveniently located and provides good service. ⓐ 19 Sharia Alfy, Downtown (Central Cairo) ⓣ (02) 591 5810 or 591 5277 ⓦ www.windsorcairo.com ⓝ Metro: Attaba

Cairo Marriott Hotel & Omar Khayyam Casino ££–£££ With sprawling grounds that include lush gardens, a swimming pool and open-air dining, this is one of the Middle East's largest hotels. Centred around a late 19th-century palace built for French Empress Eugénie's visit to the city, there are 14 dining options, an atmospheric piano bar and wonderful gardens. ⓐ 16 Sharia al-Saray al-Gezira, Zamalek (Central Cairo) ⓣ (02) 735 3000 ⓦ www.marriott.com

● *The view from a guest room at the Grand Hyatt Cairo*

Hilton Ramses ££–£££ Well located, with excellent service and a shopping arcade conveniently nearby, this is a reliable option. ⓐ 1115 Corniche el-Nil (Central Cairo) ⓣ (02) 577 7444 ⓦ www.hilton.com

Four Seasons at The First Residence £££ The many amenities of this luxury choice include airport pick-up in a BMW or Mercedes, which is handy as the location is less convenient than those in central Cairo. ⓐ 35 Sharia al-Giza, Giza (Old Cairo & Giza) ⓣ (03) 573 1212 ⓦ www.fourseasons.com

Grand Hyatt Cairo £££ Situated on the northern tip of Rhoda Island, this tower juts into the Nile and is well situated for touring around. The Revolving Restaurant, 135 m (444 ft) up, is one of the loftiest in the Middle East. ⓐ Corniche el-Nil, Rhoda Island (Central Cairo) ⓣ (02) 365 1234 ⓦ www.cairo.grand.hyatt.com

Oberoi Mena House £££ Built in 1869, this former royal hunting lodge is situated in gardens at the edge of the desert – while you'll be neighbours with the pyramids, you'll be a trek away from the centre of town and all the other sights. ⓐ Pyramids Road, Giza (Old Cairo & Giza) ⓣ (03) 377 3222 or 376 6644 ⓦ www.oberoimenahouse.com

HOSTELS
Dina's Hostel £ A six-room hostel just a few blocks from Downtown's Midan Talaat Harb – perfect for budget travelers. Free Wi-Fi. ⓐ 42 Abd El Khalek Sarwat, 5th floor, Downtown (Central Cairo) ⓣ (02) 396 3902 ⓦ www.dinashostel.com

THE BEST OF CAIRO

Whether you're ready for antiquities and hieroglyphics or you just want to discover what all the fuss is about, Cairo will delight you. There are so many must-sees that the best policy is to decide which sights are most meaningful to you and then leave a bit of room for the unexpected.

TOP 10 ATTRACTIONS

- **The Giza Pyramids** Experience the only remaining Wonder of the Ancient World (see page 89)

- **The Khan al-Khalili and Islamic Cairo** Meander through the winding streets of the bazaar and find some treasures before making your way to the Al-Azhar and Al-Hussein mosques (see page 79)

- **The Egyptian Museum** Fancy a look at Tutankhamen's Death Mask and the mummies' rooms? It would be rude not to (see page 61)

- **A felucca down the Nile** Float down the river for a different angle on the city and an afternoon chill-out (see page 43)

- ***Ahwa* culture** A few hours at a local coffee house will show you why this is a central part of Egyptian daily life (see page 16)

- **The Citadel** Gaze up at the opulent ceilings and stroll through the marble quadrangle of this reminder of the Ottoman presence (see page 74)

- **Coptic Cairo** Discover the quiet streets where the city's churches remain the central gathering points for the Coptic community (see page 84)

- **The deserts of the Sahara** Escape to the desert to clear your mind under the stars (see page 116)

- **Al-Azhar Park** Take a break in sprawling green space, with gorgeous vistas and a variety of restaurants (see pages 32 & 83)

- **Nightlife** Enjoy the uninhibited singing and fabulous dancing of the locals, not to mention the city's exciting live music scene (see page 28)

◆ *The ceiling and lamps of the Citadel*

Suggested itineraries

HALF-DAY: CAIRO IN A HURRY

Prioritise the pyramids at Giza (see page 89). They are best seen early in the morning before the sun gains full strength. Be at the ticket booth for opening at 08.00 and savour the experience at your own pace. Take a taxi to the Al-Hussein Mosque (see page 76) then wander through the Khan al-Khalili. If you have a moment, enjoy a mint tea at Fishawy's (see page 82).

1 DAY: TIME TO SEE A LITTLE MORE

After the pyramids, take a taxi to Midan Tahrir and duck into the Egyptian Museum (see page 61) for the mummies' rooms and King Tutankhamen's treasures. Once you've had your fill, head to Islamic Cairo (see page 70) then explore the area behind Al-Azhar, making your way to Beit Zeinab al-Khatoun and Beit al-Harrawi, two examples of the recent renovations of the city's Islamic architecture. In the same picturesque square you will find one of Cairo's finest artisanal craft shops, Al-Khatoun (see page 79). Finish off the day at After Eight in Downtown (see page 68).

2–3 DAYS: TIME TO SEE MUCH MORE

The first day or day-and-a-half can be spent on the above suggestions, then make your way to the Mohammed Ali Mosque in the Citadel complex (see page 74). There are a number of museums here, but if you are strapped for time, you will want to soak in the mosques here at your own pace and enjoy the view of the city from this vantage point. Make your way down from the complex and through the back streets of Old Cairo. Start your third day in

Coptic Cairo with Al-Muallaqah (Hanging Church, see page 93), where there is a wonderful indoor market. In the afternoon, hit Downtown and pick up a takeaway lunch from FelFela (see page 24). Then go through Midan Tahrir for an afternoon felucca trip down the Nile (operators line the banks). From here you are a short distance to Gezira, where you can catch sunset at the Cairo Tower (see page 56). Finish with dinner on the Nile (see page 100).

LONGER: ENJOYING CAIRO TO THE FULL

Time to explore some of Cairo's environs. The perfect post-Cairo getaway is only four hours away in the Bahariya oasis in the Sahara Desert (see page 119). A typical two- or three-day trek can be made by camel and includes a variety of desert terrain, from the undulating yellow peaks of the rock formations of the White Sands to the volcanic mountains of the Black Deserts.

● Take a camel ride while visiting the pyramids at Giza

Something for nothing

Cairo is a city that can be enjoyed on the cheap. In fact, the activities that cost the least money will probably repay you with the most authentically Cairene experiences.

You can take in the incredible sights of the city's mosques and churches for the mere price of a donation, which could give you days of thrifty exploration of the Islamic and Coptic areas. Happily, some of the best folkloric performances on offer here can be enjoyed by investing only time. Ghuri Cultural Palace (see page 77) presents an opportunity to experience one of the finest examples of restored Islamic architecture while marvelling at whirling dervishes (members of the Sufi Mevlevi Order). Ganeena Theatre (see page 77) is another great option for enjoying free live music. Seeing a show at either of these venues proves that some of the best things, in this city at least, are free.

Most of Cairo's art galleries have no admission charge. In Zamalek you can forget matters financial in places like the **Zamalek Art Gallery** (ⓐ 11 Sharia Brazil, Zamalek ⓣ (02) 735 1240 ⓦ www.zamalekartgallery.com ⓛ 09.00–21.00 Sat–Thur), which has an excellent collection of Egyptian art. Also check out the exhibits at the El Sawy Culture Wheel (see page 63). Just a short walk away from Midan Talaat Harb, you will find the **Townhouse Gallery** (ⓐ 10 Sharia Nabrawy, off Sharia Champollion ⓣ (02) 576 8086 ⓦ www.thetownhousegallery.com ⓛ 10.00–14.00, 18.00–21.00 Sat–Wed, 18.00–21.00 Fri). This is an exciting arena for creative Cairenes to display their art (and their film, drama and music), and for cost-conscious visitors to appreciate it for free. It's easy engaging with the people who run the gallery (in fact, just try keeping them away), and they'll happily tell you about the latest community development projects. If your luck's really in, they might even introduce you to an artist sitting at the shisha café on the corner.

⬤ *Exploring the busy souqs, such as Khan al-Khalili, costs nothing*

When the temperature soars

Great weather is almost guaranteed while you're here, and sometimes temperatures soar so dramatically that rushing around ticking off must-sees simply isn't an option. An easy solution is to step into a café to enjoy a fresh juice. You can also make like the locals and head for the air-conditioned City Stars (see page 78), a mega mall that offers serious shopping at an acceptable temperature. Air-conditioning may seem a rather prosaic feature to consider while you're planning your day, but, when the temperature does rocket, it will suddenly become almost as vital as oxygen. If you prefer your shopping to be more leisurely and you fancy picking up some locally made craftware, make your way to Coptic Cairo and the Souq El Fustat (see page 98) for the cool, indoor market. This area is, in general, leafy and tranquil, which is a welcome comfort under the blazing sun.

Il Pennello's ceramic café (see page 82) is a delightful refuge from the heat. If you would rather look at pottery than paint it, the Islamic Ceramic Museum (see page 63) is housed in a beautiful, airy palace. The Egyptian Museum (see page 61) is another option, although the crowds it attracts can generate a fair amount of body heat. There are plenty of opportunities to catch the breeze from the Nile, including river cruises (see page 100) and felucca rides (see page 43).

The best way to get out of the heat is to take a dip in a refreshing pool. Even if you aren't lucky enough to be staying in a 5-star hotel with a pool and deck service, that doesn't mean you can't enjoy a splash about: most of Cairo's finer hotels offer

◔ *Stay cool in the Egyptian Museum*

a day pass service for a reasonable sum. The best options are the Cairo Marriott (see page 37) and the Oberoi Mena House (see page 39). The pass will include access to the pool and fitness centre. While you're there, you might as well treat yourself to a massage as a peace offering to those no doubt tired and traumatised feet.

On arrival

TIME DIFFERENCE
Cairo is two hours ahead of Greenwich Mean Time (GMT).
Daylight Saving Time (DST) applies during the summer
months but dates vary from year to year to take account
of Ramadan.

ARRIVING
By air
Cairo International Airport (ⓐ Oruba Road, Heliopolis
ⓣ (02) 265 3308 or 268 4248 ⓦ www.cairo-airport.com) is
located in Heliopolis, 22 km (13½ miles) northeast of central
Cairo. It has full facilities, including ATMs, travel agencies and
car hire desks, and there are shuttles that operate
between terminals.

IF YOU GET LOST, TRY...

Excuse me, do you speak English?
Baad iznak/nik, betikkallim/betikkallamee ingleezee?

How do I get to ...?
Awsal le ... izay?

Can you show me on my map?
Mumkin tiraweenee 'ala il khareeta

The easiest way into town is by taxi. Official taxi services from the airport charge a flat rate of 90LE to central Cairo. An agent will carry your bag to the car, and you should tip him 3–10LE depending on how much luggage you have. Yellow and/or white metered taxis are not supposed to wait outside the airport, but if you do manage to catch one the fare should be around 60LE.

The Cairo Airport Shuttle Bus covers several locations throughout the city, with fares ranging from 25–45LE depending on your destination. However, you should pre-book this service if possible: call ☎ (02) 265 3937 or click on 'Services' then 'Transportation' on the airport website. Air-conditioned public buses also run from Terminal 1 to Downtown and other convenient locations. Bus 356 goes to Midan Tahrir, while 799 goes to Ramses. The cost of each is 2LE.

FINDING YOUR FEET

One potential culture shock could be that, as a foreigner on the streets of Cairo, you will have many people offering their services to you. While you're in areas such as Downtown in Midan Tahrir or Midan Talaat Harb, beware of touts and shopkeepers who invite you into their premises. They pose no actual danger and are merely operating their own interpretation of enterprise, but they will waste your time.

Cairo is not really the ideal place for debuting outfits that you sidelined as too risqué for your home town. It is worth considering a policy of modest dress while you're here, partly to respect the customs of the country and partly to protect yourself from unwanted attention. When visiting churches and mosques, women should cover their shoulders, and, for visits to the latter,

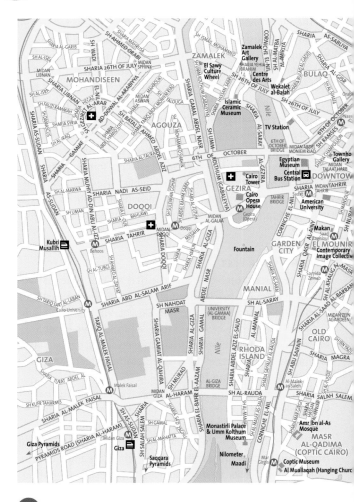

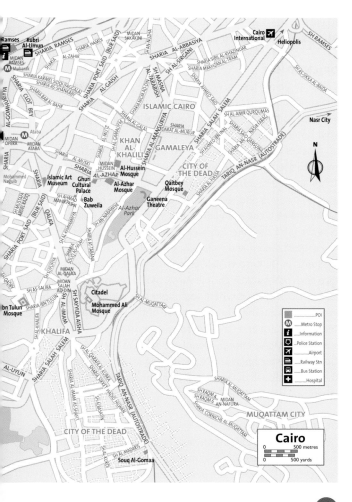

Ramses Kubri
Al-Limun
MIDAN
RAMSES
Ⓜ Mubarak

SH RAMSES

Cairo ✈
International

Heliopolis

SH RAMSES

SHARIA RAMSES

SHARIA HAMDI

MIDAN
SAKAKINI

SHARIA AL-ABBASIYA

SHARIA AL-ZAHIR

SH AL-SINGAN

SH AS-SIKKA AL-BADA

SHARIA PORT SAID (BULESAID)

SHARIA AL-GAISH

SHARIA AL-TARABISH

SHARIA SIBIL AL-KHAZINDAR

SHARIA MAK^ZAN AL-TRAM

SHARIA AL-GOMHURIYYA

SHARIA KARMEL SIDQI (FAGGALA)

SHARIA AS-SHANKABY

SHARIA BAZ AL-BAHR

SHARIA CLOT BEY

ISLAMIC CAIRO

SHARIA AHMED SAID

SHARIA AL-GALAL

SHARIA AL-MANSURIYYA

SH AL-AMIR QURQUMAS

Nasr City

Ⓜ Ataba
MIDAN
OPERA
MIDAN
ATABA

SHARIA AL-MUIZZ

SHARIA AL-GAMALIYA

SHARIA
DARAT AL-MURUR

SHARIA SALAH SALEM

SH AL-NASR (FARAG)

TARIQ AN-NASR (AUTOSTRADE)

N

SHARIA

SHARIA AL-MUSKI

KHAN
AL-
KHALILI

GAMALEYA

SHARIA SAID

SH AL-NASR

SH AHMED IBN INAL

SHARIA

Mohammed
Naguib

Islamic Art
Museum

Ghuri
Cultural
Palace

MIDAN
HUSSEIN

Al-Hussein
Mosque

CITY OF
THE DEAD

SH AHMAD
MAHIR PASHA

SH AL-AZHAR

Al-Azhar
Mosque

Qaitbey
Mosque

TARIQ AN-NASR (AUTOSTRADE)

SHARIA PORT SAID (BUR SAID)

QALAA

SH AL-KHALIJ

SHARIA AL-NABAWIYA

Bab
Zuweila

Al-Azhar
Park

Ganeena
Theatre

SHARIA AL-HASSA

SHARIA AL-TABANA

SH MUSTAFA
ABDEL RAZIQ

SHARIA

SH AS-SALIBA

SHARIA AT-TABANA

SH AL-QALAA

MIDAN
AL-QALAA

SH AL-SHINAWI

MIDAN
SALAH
AD-DIN

Citadel

Mohammed Ali
Mosque

SH AL-MUQATTAM

ibn Tulun
Mosque

SHARIA IBN TULUN

SH AL-IMAM

KHALIFA

SH SAYYIDA AISHA

SHARIA SALAH SALEM

AL-UYUN

SH AL-KHALIFA

SHARIA AL-QALAA AL-UBRA

SHARIA SIKKET HADID HIWAN

SH AL-IMAM AS-SHAFI

SH ARABSIN

TARIQ AN-NASR (AUTOSTRADE)

SHARIA AL-MUQATTAM

SH RAQM 6
SH RAQM 6
MIDAN
AN-NAFURA

SHARIA CORNICHE AL MUQATTAM

MUQATTAM CITY

CITY OF
THE DEAD

SH AL-MADARIS

SH AL-ASLAN

Souq Al-Gomaa

	POI
Ⓜ	Metro Stop
🛈	Information
Ⓟ	Police Station
✈	Airport
🚉	Railway Stn
🚌	Bus Station
✚	Hospital

Cairo
0 ──── 500 metres
0 ──── 500 yards

it will be necessary for women to cover their arms, legs and hair (there are veils on-site if you happen to forget).

ORIENTATION

Cairo can be confusing, with its winding streets, one-way thoroughfares and bewildering variety of spellings. It may be simplest to take an organised tour to begin with – just ask your hotel concierge for recommendations.

Most of the city lies on the east bank of the Nile. There is much to see and do in Downtown, where you will find Midan Tahrir and the Egyptian Museum (see page 61), an easy landmark as it is large, red and very distinctive. Across the bridge from Midan Tahrir is the island of Gezira, where Cairo's well-heeled types inhabit the elite Zamalek quarter, home to some of the city's finest dining and shopping possibilities.

South of Downtown lie Garden City and El-Mounira (which face each other across Qasr al-Ainy), Old Cairo and finally Maadi. East of Downtown is where you might lose your bearings a bit in Islamic Cairo. The whole west side of the river is called Giza. Technically, Giza and Cairo are run as separate cities, but the suburbs of Mohandiseen, Doqqi and Agouza in the Giza Governorate are areas that Cairenes regard as being part of their locale. South of Doqqi is the neighbourhood of Giza, where you will find the pyramids.

GETTING AROUND

Getting around on foot is always the best way to discover a city, and Cairo is no exception, so make sure that you are wearing comfortable footwear. The pavements are uneven and you will have to do some fancy footwork just to walk a straight line in most neighbourhoods.

Cairo's metro system is a fast, efficient way of reaching certain destinations, but it does not currently cover all parts of Cairo. To visit major areas such as Zamalek, Mohandiseen and the pyramids in Giza, you will have to hire a car or take a taxi from the closest metro station to your destination. The centre carriage of the metro is reserved for women only and is a comfortable option for female travellers on their own. The system runs smoothly and tickets are cheap; buy them at the station before boarding and hold onto them until you exit. For a map, see ⓦ www.urbanrail.net or ask at the ticket office.

Taxis are easy to hail. In summer you may want to opt for air-conditioned white (or sometimes yellow) metered cabs. While these can be more expensive than the un-metered, black-and-white taxis, any extra fare will be a small price to pay for comfort when the temperature soars.

There is always a fleet of cabs waiting in Midan Tahrir. At some destinations outside the city centre, where taxis are not so prevalent, it's worthwhile getting the driver to wait for you.

There are a few taxi tips to keep in mind: women should sit in the back seat; only the passenger's side door of the back seat will

🔺 *Cairo Metro sign*

open; when you pay the driver, it is best to pass him the money through the window when you're outside the vehicle. If he argues for additional money and you are certain that you have paid him fairly, simply walk away.

The city's buses and minibuses are the locals' main mode of transportation, but the extremely cramped ride is avoided by all those who can afford other options. Destinations are marked in Arabic and can be difficult to decipher unless you are familiar with the routes.

❶ We have included public transport details for sights and venues where the metro is a practical option. If no public transport option is listed, this means it's best to walk or take a taxi.

CAR HIRE

While hiring a car is not your best option for getting around Cairo, it's very useful for excursions out of town. Some reputable companies are:

Avis ❸ 16A Sharia Ma'amal el-Sukar, Garden City ❶ (02) 279 2400; Airport Terminal 1 ❶ (02) 265 4249 and Terminal 2 ❶ (02) 265 2429 ❿ www.avisegypt.com

Budget ❸ 22 Sharia el-Muthaf al-Zira'i, Doqqi ❶ (03) 762 0518; Airport Terminal 2 ❶ (02) 265 2395 ❿ www.budget.com

Hertz ❸ 195 Sharia 26th of July, Agouza ❶ (02) 347 4172; Airport Terminal 2 ❶ (02) 265 2430 ❿ www.hertzegypt.com

---

❿ *View down the Nile*

THE CITY OF
Cairo

Central Cairo

Central Cairo includes the bustling streets of Downtown, the elegant restaurants and galleries of Zamalek and the congested (but lively) suburb of Mohandiseen. Coursing right through the centre of it all is the Nile, on whose banks you can stop for a break to watch fishermen and feluccas. This is the hub of Cairene life: you'll find everything here, from the elite American University in Cairo in Midan Tahrir to the street pedlars and their various wares dotting the Corniche and Downtown streets. You can plan to spend a day discovering all of the nooks and crannies of these neighbourhoods, or pick out different quarters for different days. Either way, you won't be disappointed. As a rule of thumb, the action is to be found in Downtown by day, but in the evening you may prefer to head to Zamalek for an upmarket dinner and show.

SIGHTS & ATTRACTIONS

Cairo Tower

Said to imitate the appearance of a lotus plant, this tower in the centre of Cairo is 187 m (613 ft) high and offers wonderful panoramic views. If you've got the stomach for it, try the revolving restaurant, where you'll be able to savour the vista from every angle. ⓐ Sharia Hadayek al-Zuhreya ⓣ (02) 735 7187 ⓛ 08.00–00.00 ⓝ Metro: Gezira. Admission charge

---

⦿ *Cairo Tower*

Central Cairo

0 _____ 500 metres
0 _____ 500 yards

SHARIA AS-SUDAN

SHARIA EL-NIL

SHARIA EL-ALAMEIN

SH RASHID

SHARIA AHMED ORABI

SHARIA AL-MASHRU

MIDAN
AL-KIT KAT

SHARIA AL-GARIB

SHAMA MAHRUSA

SHARIA MOHAMMED MARAGHI

SHARIA ABU AL-FEDA

SHOHAMMED MARAGHI

SHARIA AL-ISRA

SHARIA WADI EL-NIL

SHARIA MOHAMMED BADR AD-DIN

ZAMALEK

SHARIA AL-MASHRU

SHARIA 26TH

SHARIA 26TH OF JULY

MIDAN
OF SPHINX

0①

SHARIA AL-MAKSHY

SH. TAHA HUSSEIN

0④

El Sawy
Culture
Wheel

0⑪ **0**⑥

Egyptian Centre for
International
Cultural
Cooperation

0⑭ **0**⑫

0⑯

Centre
des Arts

0②

Islamic
Ceramic
Museum

MIDAN
LIBNAN

SHARIA 26TH OF JULY

MOHANDISEEN

HEGAZ

SHARIA GEZIRET AL-ARAB

AD-DUWAL

MIDAN
ASWAN

MAHROUR

SHARIA FALOUGA

SHARIA GAMAL ABDEL NASR

SHARIA AL-SARAY
AL-GEZIRA

SHARIA AL-ISRA

SHARIA FAUZI RAMMAH

SHARIA DAMASCUS

SHARIA SYRIA

SHARIA IRAQ

GAMIINT

SHARIA ABDEL HAMID LOTFY

SHARIA TANG

SHARIA BATAL AHMED ABDEL AZIZ

SHARIA ABDEL MONIM RIAD

SHARIA AL-SHISHINI

SHARIA MOHAMMED MAZHAR

AGOUZA

SHARIA KOTHUM (GABALEYA)

SHARIA SALAH SALEM

SHARIA GEZIRET AL-ARAB

SHARIA AL-TAIRA

SHARIA UMM KOLTHUM

SHARIA AS-SUDAN

SHARIA MUHIY AD-DIN ABUL-IZZ

6TH OF OCTOBER

SH HASSAN
MOHAMMED AL-RAZZA

Cairo Tower

SHARIA HADAYEK AL-ZUHREYA

SH MAHMUD

GEZIRA

MUKHTA

SHARIA NADI AS-SEID

SHARIA AL-MARWA

SHARIA UMAN

DOQQI

SHARIA OUR BAHLAWI

SHARIA SULEIMAN GOHAR

SHARIA ABDEL RAHIM SABRI

SH ABD EL-AZIZ

SHARIA SADAT ALY

Cairo
Opera
House

SHARIA UMM KOLTHUM (GABALEYA)

M TAHRIR

Gezira
(Opera)

SHARIA TAHRIR

MIDAN
AL-GALAA

SHARIA AL-GIZA

SHARIA TAHRIR

MIDAN
DOQQI

SH AMIN BEY AR-RAFI

M Doqqi

SHARIA AL-TUBGI

M Behoos

SHARIA AHMED ZAKI

SHARIA DOQQI

Fountain

Nile

MANIAL

	POI
M	Metro Stop
i	Information
	Police Station
✈	Airport
	Railway Stn
	Bus Station
✚	Hospital

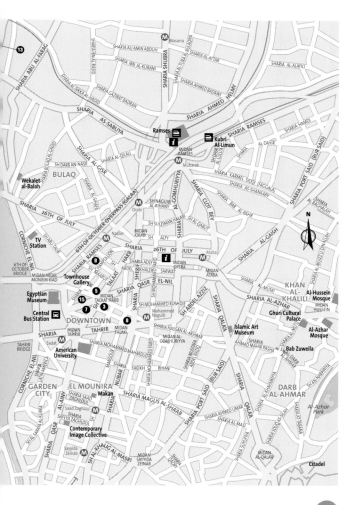

LOVERS OF THE NILE

Don't be fooled by cultural stereotypes of gender segregation in the region. While families here may exert a little more influence over youngsters' love-lives than they do in the West, all it takes is a stroll down the Corniche (or promenade) and the bridges joining Gezira to the mainland to see that Cairo's young lovers enjoy a walk by the river as much as their Parisian counterparts on the Seine. A mix of married and unmarried couples, they come to enjoy the fresh air of the river and the anonymity of the crowds.

CULTURE

Cairo Opera House

This multiplex includes a variety of theatres and resources for those looking to enjoy the highest end of Cairo's cultural scene. There are scores of musical and theatrical options for visitors, from the local performances in the Small Hall to the grand performances of the Cairo Opera Company in the Main Hall.
ⓐ Sharia Tahrir, Gezira ☏ (02) 739 0114 or 739 8114
ⓦ www.cairoopera.org Ⓜ Metro: Gezira

Centre des Arts

The exhibits of this centre, which came about as a result of a government initiative, are displayed in a beautiful old villa.

A number of shows are put on annually, including the Youth Salon, a peek into which will give an accurate flavour of the local modern art scene. ⓐ 1 Maahad al-Swissri, Zamalek ⓣ (02) 735 8211

Contemporary Image Collective

With rotating exhibits and darkroom facilities, this is Cairo's haven for photographers and photography lovers. ⓐ 20 Sharia Safeya Zaghloul, El Mounira ⓣ (02) 794 1686 ⓦ www.ciccairo.com ⓛ 10.00–19.00 Sun–Thur ⓝ Metro: Saad Zaghloul

Egyptian Centre for International Cultural Cooperation

The title says it all. Another result of a government-administered programme, the centre offers a wide variety of lectures, exhibitions, recitals, films and even excursions. ⓐ 11 Sharia Shagaret ad-Durr, Zamalek ⓣ (02) 341 5419 ⓛ 09.30–22.00 Sat–Thur

Egyptian Museum

Built between 1897 and 1900, this museum is filled with a mass of archaeological finds that mostly date back more than 5,000 years. From mummies to the golden treasures of Pharaohs, tools, urns and more, a wander through this museum will give you a glimpse of the rich history of Egypt. Prioritise the Tutankhamen galleries on the first floor, and make a similarly determined beeline for the BBC Galleries, whose photo collection is a potent appetiser for the delights that lie within. ⓐ Midan Tahrir ⓣ (02) 578 2448 or 578 2452 ⓛ 09.00–17.45 ⓝ Metro: Sadat. Admission charge

Islamic Ceramic Museum

Housed in the Gezira Art Center complex, the Islamic Ceramic Museum displays over 300 urns, plates and other fine pieces dating from the 10th to the 19th centuries. The building is a palace that was completed in 1343, and exhibits are beautifully displayed throughout the ambient space. ⓐ 1 Sharia Sheikh al-Marsafy, Zamalek (entrance off Sharia al-Saray al-Gezira) ⓣ (02) 737 3298 ⓛ 10.00–13.30, 17.00–21.00 ⓝ Metro: Gezira

Makan

For live music and a look at some of Cairo's most talented musicians, head to Makan. Many performances at this cherished gathering place of the city's artistic community highlight the talents of African refugees. ⓐ 1 Sharia Saad Zaghloul, El Mounira ⓣ (02) 792 0878 ⓦ www.egyptmusic.org ⓝ Metro: Saad Zaghloul

El Sawy Culture Wheel

This unique space, built underneath the 15th of May Bridge on the Nile, offers programming that ranges from puppet shows to traditional *oud* (a musical instrument like a lute) performances, hip-hop and an annual chocolate festival. An unexpected bonus is the variety of people you'll find wandering among the exhibits. Explanatory material is available in English, French and German. ⓐ Sharia 26th of July, under 15th of May Bridge, Zamalek ⓣ (02) 736 8881 ⓦ http://culturewheel.com

◀ *Tutankhamen's treasures on show at the Egyptian Museum*

RETAIL THERAPY

Azza Fahmy Celebrated Egyptian jewellery designer Azza Fahmy makes wonderful designs out of silver. 15C Sharia Taha Hussein, corner Sharia Al-Marashly, Zamalek 🕿 (02) 2735 8354 🕐 10.00–22.00 Ⓜ Metro: Gezira

Diwan One of Cairo's largest bookstores, its selection of English, French and Arabic titles and CDs echoes the owners' friendly, international outlook. Culture buffs will be excited by an extensive collection that covers the politics, history, religion and literature of the region. 159 Sharia 26th of July 🕿 (02) 736 2582 🕐 09.00–00.30 Ⓜ Metro: Gezira

Fair Trade Company An excellent selection of items from bags and baskets to loofahs and ponchos, all at very good prices, makes this shop a favourite with Egyptians and visitors alike. 27 Sharia Yehia Ibrahim 🕿 (02) 736 5123 🌐 www.fairtradeegypt.org 🕐 11.00–00.00 Ⓜ Metro: Gezira

El Gozour Centre It is easy to find music kiosks across town selling chart-toppers, Western tunes and Egyptian films, but the eclectic range of fare on offer here makes this shop a music lovers' and film fans' paradise. 163 Sharia 26th of July 🕿 (03) 346 6774 🕐 10.00–00.00

O-M Art Gallery A small shop tucked just off Shagarat el-Dorr, this sparkling find boasts leather collage works, lighting fixtures, jewellery and vibrant tapestries. The owners are incredibly friendly and can make items to suit your tastes. 🅐 14 Sharia Hassan Assem, Zamalek 🅣 (02) 736 3165 🅛 11.00–22.00 🅝 Metro: Gezira

Oum El Dounia Popular among tourists, this shop sells local glass, jewellery, lamps and other treasures for the home, as well as a French-inspired take on lush Oriental bedding and clothing. 🅐 3 Sharia Talaat Harb, Downtown 🅣 (02) 393 8273 🅛 09.00–21.00 🅝 Metro: Sadat

Al-Qahira Traditional Egyptian design meets superb modern craftwork – perfect for a gift or elegant souvenir. 🅐 6 Sharia Bahgat Ali, 2nd floor, Zamalek 🅣 011 313 3932 🅛 11.00–21.00 Mon–Sat 🅝 Metro: Gezira

TAKING A BREAK

Arabica £ ❶ Sample the inventive juices (such as strawberry with a dash of balsamic vinegar) with a savoury *fiteer*. Good service and a hip, modern atmosphere. 🅐 20 Sharia Al-Marashly, Zamalek 🅣 (02) 735 7982 🅛 10.00–02.00

Beano's £ ❷ With a few Beano's to choose from in Central Cairo, your best bet is to head to the Zamalek branch, where the second-floor view of the garden behind the Islamic Ceramic Museum will provide a lofty, perhaps even refined, break in your day. 🅐 Midan El Sheikh al-Marsafy, off Sharia 26th of July 🅣 (02) 736 2388 🅛 07.00–01.00 🅝 Metro: Gezira

Café Riche £ ❸ An old favourite of the city's arty types and

intellectuals, these days it can be a challenge to find the joint open. If you do, you'll be pleased you did; if you don't, a gander at the nostalgic décor will still make the trip worthwhile.
ⓐ 17 Sharia Talaat Harb, Downtown ⓣ (02) 392 9793 or 391 8873
ⓛ 11.00–23.30 ⓝ Metro: Sadat

Cilantro £ ❹ The Egyptian answer to Starbucks. Started by graduates of the American University, this coffee shop is always packed with young, well-groomed Cairenes. ⓐ 7 Sharia Abu al-Feda ⓣ (02) 736 5628 ⓛ 24 hrs

Groppi £ ❺ Once the most celebrated tearooms this side of the Mediterranean and the setting of many an Egyptian romantic movie, Groppi's is worn-in and well-loved. Choose from cases of sweets or from the sandwich menu. The food is fine, but the

● *Try the sweetened figs, dates and grapes at Groppi*

visit is really more about glimpsing its former glory. ⓐ Midan Talaat Harb, Downtown ⓛ 07.00–00.00 Ⓜ Metro: Sadat

Mandarin Koueidar £ ❻ The place the locals head to for their trays of Egyptian sweets before going to a dinner party. Stand in front of counters of sumptuous Oriental treats and just point to your favourites. They also serve the best gelato in town. ⓐ 17 Sharia Shagaret ad-Durr, Zamalek ⓣ (02) 735 5010 ⓛ 12.00–23.00 Ⓜ Metro: Gezira

Estoril ££ ❼ This is your chance to see some of Cairo's artists as they stop in for a beer and *sambousek* (fried stuffed pastry). In general, Estoril attracts a mixed crowd of foreigners and the city's bohemians. ⓐ 17 Sharia Talaat Harb, Downtown ⓣ (02) 574 3102 ⓛ 12.00–00.00 Ⓜ Metro: Sadat

AFTER DARK

Horreya £ ❽ This drinking hole is legendary for its eclectic clientele, cheap beer and never-ending games of backgammon. Fluorescently lit, high-ceilinged and dotted with the odd mirror, this basic boozer will introduce you to Cairo's drinking scene, and to a few of its notable characters. ⓐ Midan Falaki, Downtown ⓛ From 10.00 (hours vary) Ⓜ Metro: Sadat

Odeon Palace Bar £ ❾ A 24-hour rooftop bar. A great place to relax with a drink and a shisha. ⓐ Odeon Palace Hotel, 6 Sharia Abdel Hamid, off Sharia Ramses, Downtown ⓣ (02) 579 65117 ⓛ 24 hrs Ⓜ Metro: Sadat

Cairo Jazz Club ££ This is the heart of Cairo's live music scene. The jazz situation isn't world class, but you can find the city's most popular bands, hear some innovative sounds and have a memorable night out. @ 197 Sharia 26th of July, Agouza ☎ (03) 345 9939 🕐 19.00–03.00

Pub 28 ££ This typical British pub is frequented by expats and Egyptians alike and offers local and international brands of alcohol as well as a decent food menu. Open during Ramadan. @ 28 Sharia Shagaret ad-Durr, Zamalek ☎ (02) 012 214 8637 🕐 12.00–02.00 Ⓜ Metro: Gezira

L'Aubergine ££–£££ Vegetarians will be pleased to find that Cairo does, in fact, do vegetarian restaurants. This is one of the very few. @ 5 Sharia El Sayed Bakry, off Sharia 26th of July, Zamalek ☎ (02) 738 0080 🕐 Restaurant: 10.00–02.00; bar: 19.30–02.00

Absolute £££ Have some grub then dance with a spiffy crowd in this hip spot on the Nile. Very good food that just about justifies the prices. @ Corniche el-Nil, Bulaq ☎ (02) 579 6512 🕐 12.00–03.00

Abu el-Sid £££ Excellent, authentic cuisine served in an atmosphere of an Egyptian upper-class salon with a modern twist. Always packed, so make a reservation. @ Sharia El Sayed Bakry, off Sharia Brazil, Zamalek ☎ (02) 735 9640 🕐 12.00–02.00 Ⓜ Metro: Gezira

After Eight £££ The night starts off with dining on dips, but as it gets later, the music gets louder, the tables get pushed to the

🔺 *Dining at La Bodega*

side and you will experience Cairo's live music and club scene at its most exuberant. The city's best bands cram onto the tiny stage regularly, so be sure to make reservations. ⓐ 6 Sharia Qasr el-Nil, Downtown ⓘ (02) 339 8000 ⓛ 20.00–03.00 Sun–Wed, 20.00–04.00 Thur–Sat ⓜ Metro: Sadat

La Bodega £££ ⓰ With a restaurant, bar and lounge, this is the quintessential Zamalek food-and-fun night spot, with a smart crowd and neat eats. ⓐ 157 Sharia 26th of July, Zamalek ⓘ (02) 735 0543 ⓛ 12.00–01.00

Sequoia £££ ⓱ A spacious outdoor patio on the Nile, with a DJ and superb food. ⓐ End of Sharia Abu al-Feda, Zamalek ⓘ (02) 735 0014 ⓛ 12.00–01.00 ⓜ Metro: Gezira

Islamic Cairo

The attractions of this part of town include bewitching mosques and the delights of souq shopping. Walking through Islamic Cairo, it is easy to imagine what the old city must have looked like, thanks to the scores of minarets. As donkey-carts roll by, allow yourself to get lost in the alleyways and passages. An earthquake in 1992 damaged many of the area's buildings, and this brought to everybody's attention the need to renovate their fine Islamic architecture. This is an ongoing process, and from the Al-Azhar's minaret you can see the uneven (and sometimes decidedly tilted) appearance of many of the buildings below.

🔻 *Al-Azhar Park*

Close to Islamic Cairo are the broad avenues of Heliopolis and Nasr City, home to the City Stars mall (see page 78) and Cairo National Stadium (see page 32). The closest metro station to Islamic Cairo is Attaba on line 2. Depending on your destination, you may have to walk a fair distance from here or take a taxi.

SIGHTS & ATTRACTIONS

Al-Azhar Mosque

The Al-Azhar Mosque is a grand structure that reflects many centuries of architectural styles. The 15th-century entrance gate and the original 10th-century Fatimid façade of the courtyard are examples of how this mosque was developed over the years. If you are lucky enough to have one of the local tour guides spot

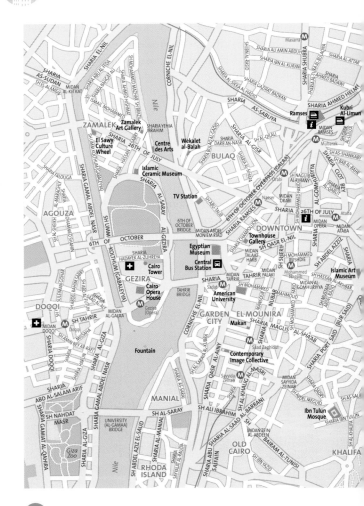

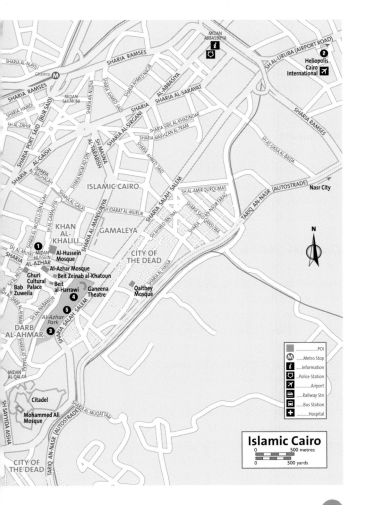

Islamic Cairo

0   500 metres
0   500 yards

POI
Metro Stop
Information
Police Station
Airport
Railway Stn
Bus Station
Hospital

you, he'll explain all the major features, including the tomb of the revered Islamic scholar, Imam el-Shafi'I (c. AD 800). Allow your guide to give you a hand up the minarets and enjoy one of the best views in Cairo (incidentally, a 50LE tip is appropriate for this sort of service). ⓐ Sharia Al-Azhar ⓛ Open daily; avoid prayer times (particularly Fridays)

Bab Zuweila

This beautiful tenth-century gate is the only remaining southern portal of Cairo. In Mameluke times, it was a major gathering point as the site of street theatre and public executions. The two minarets at the top are those of the Mosque of al-Mu'ayyad, and they can be climbed for fantastic views. ⓷ Sharia al-Darb al-Ahmar

Citadel (Al-Qala'a) & Mohammed Ali Mosque

The site is made up of more than a dozen buildings, including mosques and museums, all of which are centred on the stunning Mohammed Ali Mosque. In 1168, Saladin began making plans for the defence of Cairo; an exquisite citadel, built to the most advanced construction techniques of the time, was the major component. For 700 years Al-Qala'a (the Citadel) represented the central symbolic and defensive point of Egypt's rulers. Sadly, nothing remains of the original fortress except a part of the exterior walls.

The Mohammed Ali Mosque is one of Cairo's most famous postcard images and can be seen perched on its hill from many parts of the city. Its high ceilings and incredible chandeliers are notably different from anything else found in the city's mosques, bearing as they do the influence of the Ottoman style of

◆ *The Citadel*

architecture. The Citadel's Al-Gawhara Theatre is a great place to experience the whirling dervishes of the Sufi tradition. Queue at the exit gate of the Citadel and make sure you're there early to be able to attend the **free show** (🕐 19.00 Mon, Wed, Sat, winter; 20.00 Mon, Wed, Sat, summer. ➌ Midan Al-Qala'a ☎ (02) 512 1735 🕐 08.00–17.00 Oct–May; 08.00–18.00 June–Sept

Al-Hussein Mosque

Across the street from the Al-Azhar Mosque (see page 71), the Al-Hussein includes a mausoleum for what are claimed to be

AN ISLAMIC EDUCATION

Al-Azhar University is one of the oldest operating academic establishments in the world. Actually, it claims to be the oldest Islamic university, although this is disputed by the Kairaouine Mosque in Fes, Morocco. The mosque and university are named after the Prophet Muhammad's daughter, Fatima Az-Zahraa. The school of theology was founded in AD 988 as an Ismaili Shia school, but later became a Sunni school and has remained so to this day. Al-Azhar is considered by most Sunnis to be the most prestigious school of Islamic law, and its scholars are respected by Muslims worldwide. In addition to law, the university originally focused on literature, astronomy, philosophy and Arabic grammar. Over the years, the curriculum has expanded to include such departments as Engineering. The original building is located beside Al-Azhar Mosque (see page 71), while a larger campus is now in Nasr City.

the remains of the Prophet Muhammad's grandson, Hussein. Officially the mosque is closed to non-Muslims, but you may be able to peek inside when prayers are not underway; the women's entrance is opposite the Khan al-Khalili (see page 79). ⓐ Sharia Al-Azhar

Ibn Tulun Mosque

This mosque is credited as being the third-largest in the world (and, in its original incarnation, the oldest in Egypt). Ibn Tulun built it in 879 to accommodate his army during Friday prayers, and it was the centre of al-Qatai, the capital of his dynasty. The minaret is modelled on the style of the famous mosque in Samarra, with its spiralling staircase on the outside of the tower. Another notable feature is an expansive courtyard that's studded with an enormous sycamore frieze that includes verses from the Quran. ⓐ Sharia Ibn Tulun, Khalifa 🕐 09.00–17.00. Admission charge

CULTURE

Ganeena Theatre

Nestled inside Al-Azhar Park on the side overlooking Darb Al-Ahmar, this theatre has stunning views of Darb Al-Ahmar and the Ayyubid wall that was uncovered in creating the gardens. Check out local listings for regular live music performances. ⓐ Al-Azhar Park, Sharia Salah Salem, Darassa ☎ (02) 575 5191

Ghuri Cultural Palace

Initially intended as an inn for traders, the building was erected in 1504 by the Sultan Qunsuwah Al Ghouri. The beautiful

CITIES OF THE DEAD

Walking through the Cities of the Dead on the eastern side of the city will reveal the five sprawling cemeteries that have been taken over by those who are too poor to afford Cairo's housing. An estimated 600,000 people live among the tombs, existing without electricity or water. If you do decide to explore these neighbourhoods, do be aware that the Ministry of Tourism closed key tourist attractions in the cemeteries, including the Qaitbey Mosque, to dissuade foreigners from venturing in. Be careful walking on the uneven ground here and dress conservatively. Women may even wish to cover their hair simply to attract less attention and thus explore more freely. Do be respectful of the people and the space that they have made their home.

architecture remains today and is enjoyed by visitors who come to appreciate the extensive arts programming. Home to an artisans' market, if you come here in the evening you'll find whirling dervish displays (Wednesday and Saturday in summer) and Arabic music concerts. Performances are free, so arrive early. ⓐ Qasr al-Ghuri, off Sharia al-Mu'iz, Islamic Cairo ⓣ (02) 506 0227 ⓛ From 09.00 (hours vary)

RETAIL THERAPY

City Stars With 800 stores that are a mix of high-end international brands and local selections, this shopping centre also includes an enormous indoor theme park, a multiplex cinema and an excellent food court. It truly rivals the renowned malls of Dubai for retail premiership in the region. Its sheer enormity may tire you out, but there are plenty of café and dining options if you need them. This is a glimpse of Egypt's rapidly expanding market for imported luxuries, as well as a fun place for checking out how tastefully the city's upper classes exercise their purchasing power. ⓐ Golden Pyramids Plaza, 2 Sharia Aly Rashad, Heliopolis ⓣ (02) 480 0500 ⓛ 10.00–00.00 ⓦ www.citystars.com.eg

Khan al-Khalili Since the 14th century the Khan al-Khalili has buzzed with commercial activity. This is a maze of small streets, narrow alleys and passages filled with scores of vendors hawking their wares and attempting to draw customers into their tiny shops with such subtly enticing lines as 'Come here and let me show you how I take your money'. With a little determination, you can find gold and silver jewellery, leather work, glassware, fabrics, spices and, perhaps, that perfect gift for yourself. ⓐ Behind Al-Hussein Mosque, off Sharia al-Azhar ⓛ 10.00–22.00 Mon–Sat; most shops close Sun and during Fri prayer

Khan Misr Toulun In front of the Ibn Tulun Mosque you will find this small, quirky store selling handicrafts from all over Egypt. These high-quality items run from shawls to dolls, wooden chests and glass and are all marked with price tags if you are not up for haggling in the markets. It's a great place to find quality souvenirs and gifts for family and friends at home. ⓐ Sharia Ibn Tulun, Khalifa ⓣ (02) 365 2227 ⓛ 10.00–17.00 (closed Sat & Sun in Aug)

Al-Khatoun Located in the renovated quarter of Darb Al-Ahmar, this is a must-visit gift shop. Explore the huge collection of tunics, copper lamps and chandeliers, pottery, kitsch cinema posters, furniture and delicately hand-painted mirrors. Their jewellery case is essential for locating original pieces and the intricately latticed copper coasters are easy to carry home as gifts. ⓐ 3 Sharia Muhammad Abdouh, behind Al-Azhar Mosque

⬤ *The enormous City Stars*

☎ (02) 514 7164 Ⓦ www.alkhatoun.net 🕐 11.00–21.00 (until 00.00 during Ramadan)

Sharia al-Muski After you finish with the souvenirs at the Khan al-Khalili you can make your way down Sharia al-Muski to see the little shops where Egyptians buy their daily wares, from shoes to underwear and everything in between. ⓐ Perpendicular to Sharia al-Azhar

Sharia Qala'a For traditional musical instruments, this street has several shops to choose from. You can see the workshops where the instruments are crafted, and in these you will find the *kanoon* (dulcimer), the *oud* (lute), *nai* (flute) *rabab* (viol) and, of course, the *tabla*, the hand drum that keeps dancers shaking. ⓐ Between Midan Ataba and the Islamic Art Museum

TAKING A BREAK

Fishawy's £ ❶ After haggling in the Khan al-Khalili you might well want to sit back and chill in the magical Fishawy's. You'll be alone among a never-ending stream of tourists and locals. Vendors selling necklaces and other portable items can be rather aggressive, but won't bother you if you don't make eye contact. The café has every possible drink on offer, as well as decent shisha. The real pulls here are the ornate wood, the aged (but still opulent) chandeliers and the lively atmosphere. ⓐ 37 Sharia al-Fishawy, off Sharia al-Muski (near Al-Hussein Hotel), Khan al-Khalili 🕑 24 hrs (except Ramadan)

Il Pennello ££ ❷ This beautiful villa-turned-café/restaurant is just the place for anyone who wants to unleash their creative energies. Choose from the many plain ceramic pieces, get your palette of colours and simply create magic while you enjoy one of their great coffees or hearty lunches. You'll then be ready to head out into the city again for fresh inspiration. ⓐ 2 Sharia Omar Ibn Al-Khattab and Sharia Abu Bakr al-Seddiq, Heliopolis ⓣ (02) 241 7603 🕑 09.00–01.00

AFTER DARK

Al-Azhar Park restaurants ££ If you need to escape from the city's crowds and hawkers, the restaurants at Al-Azhar Park – Lakeside Café **❸**, Alain la Notre **❹** and Trianon **❺** – will give you some respite. A late afternoon walk through the gardens will get you ready for the sunset and a Lebanese dinner at the Lakeside Café, or for Trianon's lunch, dinner and dessert menus.

⬤ *Take a break at Fishawy's*

Old Cairo & Giza

Stretching from Rhoda Island to Coptic Cairo and the Giza pyramids, this area spans the southern part of Cairo. Garden City, an upmarket neighbourhood that has fallen into disrepair, was designed using gardens and spiralling streets to keep out the 'riffraff' and ensure that only locals would be capable of navigating its winding avenues. Further south, Masr al-Qadima may translate as 'Old Cairo', but it actually refers to Coptic Cairo and its environs. This area can be reached easily by metro – all you

need to do is get out at the Mar Girgis Station, where you can stroll along the quiet street that was once home to 20 churches. The five that remain are a must-see while you're in town. Just down the road from them you'll find the earliest mosque ever built in Africa.

In Giza, at the edge of the sprawling city, are the pyramids. Many visitors only make time for these, but if you have an extra couple of hours, it is also well worth exploring Saqqara, where you will find the famous Step Pyramid (see page 94).

◯ *The Sphinx*

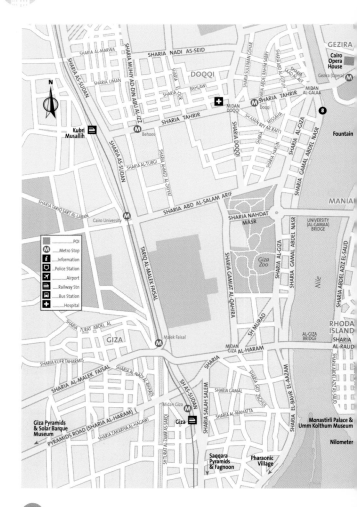

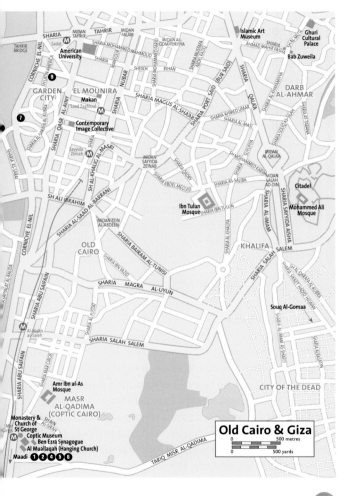

EGYPTOLOGY TODAY

Egyptology is a popular academic field and Dr. Zahi Hawass, Secretary-General for the Supreme Council on Antiquities, is one of its most well-known exponents. A fierce warrior in the fight to regain plundered Egyptian antiquities, he is regarded by some as the most knowledgeable and experienced academic in his field. Hawass is author of several internationally successful books, including *King Tutankhamun: The Treasures of the Tomb*, *The Curse of the Pharaohs: My Adventures with Mummies* and *The Hidden Treasure of the Egyptian Museum*. His website (ⓦ http://drhawass.com) is entertaining and informative and a good place to prepare for your visits to the country's ancient historical sites.

SIGHTS & ATTRACTIONS

Amr Ibn al-As Mosque

Built in 642 by the commander of the Muslim army that brought Islam to Egypt, this was the first mosque in Africa. The original structure consisted of columns made from split palm tree trunks and mud bricks, covered by a roof of wood and leaves. It was destroyed in 1169 to prevent the Crusaders from capturing it, but after they were expelled Saladin took power and had the mosque rebuilt in 1179. Today it accommodates some of the city's largest congregations during Ramadan prayers.

ⓐ Sharia Mar Girgis ⓜ Metro: Mar Girgis

Ben Ezra Synagogue

Originally a Christian church, the building was sold in 882 to
Jewish writer and thinker Abraham Ibn Ezra. It soon became
a central point for Egypt's Jewish community. The present
building dates from 1892 and is a reconstruction of the original;
a highly significant consequence of this reconstruction was
the discovery of thousands of sacred books and Torah scrolls
dating from the Middle Ages. The documents are currently
at Cambridge University, where researchers are discovering
new information about Jewish culture in the region and
their relations with Muslims at the time. ⓐ Sharia Mar Girgis
Ⓜ Metro: Mar Girgis

Fagnoon

This is a place for children to enjoy drawing, making jewellery
or simply playing in the garden while their parents have a go at
making bread in a mud-brick stove. There is a small greenhouse,
as well as options for children to ride horses, donkeys or camels.
You'll have to take a taxi to get here; on your return, ask staff
to call one for you. ⓐ Sakkara Road, Sabil Om Hashim, Giza
ⓣ (03) 815 1633 ⓦ www.fagnoon.net ⓛ 09.00–17.00

Giza Pyramids

The 4,000 year-old-Giza pyramids include the Pyramid of Khufu
(also known as the Great Pyramid or Pyramid of Cheops), the
Pyramid of Khafre and the Pyramid of Menkaure. Additionally,
you will find three smaller pyramids south of the main headliners.
These are thought to have been practice efforts, constructed as
rehearsals for the real deal. The stunning size of these edifices

GREAT PYRAMIDS SOUND & LIGHT SHOW

While the commentary is less than inspiring and the whole extravaganza may teeter on the edge of kitsch, an evening in the desert air with the light show on the Sphinx and Pyramids is a unique and enjoyable experience. ☎ (02) 386 3469 or 385 2880 or 285 4509 🌐 www.soundandlight.com.eg 🕐 Shows: 18.30, 19.30, 20.30 winter; 20.30, 21.30, 22.30 summer (but call to check) Ⓜ Metro: Midan Giza, then a taxi. Admission charge

is enough to leave spectators in awe – the Pyramid of Khufu includes 2.3 million blocks.

The pyramids were constructed as gigantic tombs for the Pharaohs, though there is much debate as to how they were actually put together and who exactly built them. Findings by academics Zahi Hawass (see page 88) and Mark Lehner revealed the quarters where the ancient Egyptian workers were housed; it is now believed that they were not slaves as originally believed, but an organised specialist workforce. These discoveries cast new light not only on the building of the pyramids but on the entire civilisation of ancient Egypt.

You can go inside the Great Pyramid, and if you are not claustrophobic it is a wonderful experience to get the inside view of the incredible structure. Access is limited, with just two rounds of tickets issued in the morning and afternoon.

The mysterious Great Sphinx structure is called Abu al-Hol in Arabic, which translates as 'Father of Terror'. It is the largest monolithic statue in the world, with a height of 73.5 m (241 ft) and a width of 6 m (20 ft). Believed to have been built in the third millennium BC, it is credited as being the earliest sculpture in human history.

Be prepared for aggressive touts, so if you do not wish to ride a camel or buy a postcard, make sure you charge forward without making eye contact with the vendors. Also, if you are taking a taxi to the pyramids, tell the driver that you will pay him when you are in front of the ticket office. It is not uncommon for drivers to drop their passengers off in the hands of camel drivers or perfume and carpet factory owners who give them tips for delivering potential clients. Being firm and insisting that you see the ticket sales booth will ensure that you are not railroaded into an unwanted – and possibly anti-climactic – tour of a factory.

● *The stepped Saqqara Pyramids (see page 94)*

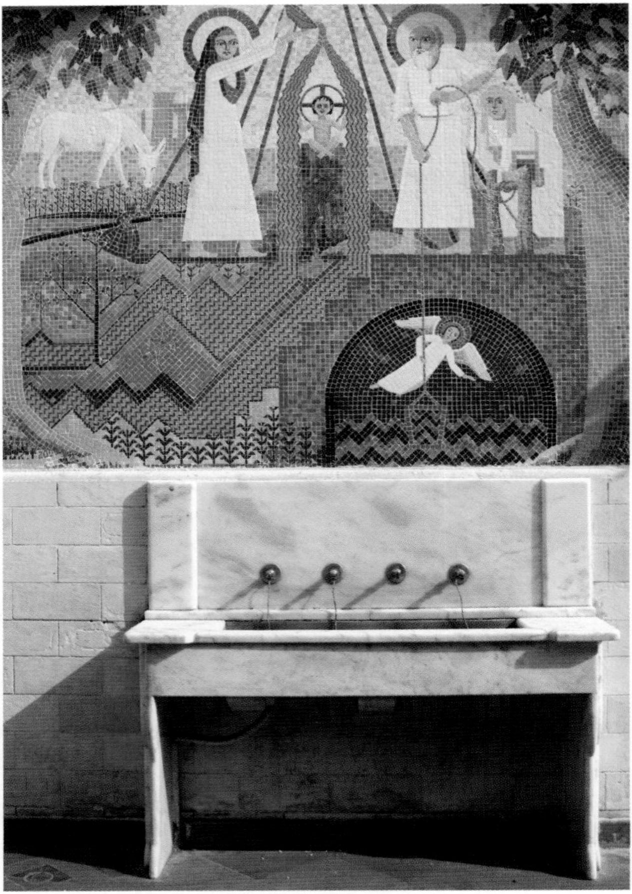

Bright mosaics in the courtyard of the Hanging Church

ⓐ Giza Plateau ⏱ 09.00–16.30 Ⓜ Metro: Midan Giza, then taxi to pyramids (a taxi from Downtown is easier and should cost around 40LE). Admission charge

Giza Zoo

Appreciated by grateful locals as an expanse of green in the middle of town, this somewhat outdated zoo houses a mix of animals, including pink storks, white flamingos, a sad-looking elephant and several monkeys, some of which are in distressing states of health. To allow the city's poorer citizens to have a chance to see the gardens and the animals, the zoo charges only a quarter of an Egyptian pound for entrance; this is not even enough to cover operating costs, which may explain its current disrepair. ⓐ Midan Nahdet Misr ⏱ 09.00–17.00 Ⓜ Metro: Doqqi. Admission charge

Monastery & Church of St George

The principal Greek Orthodox church in Egypt, the church of St George (of dragon-slaying fame) was built in the tenth century. A fire destroyed the original structure and the building that now stands is the 1904 reconstruction. The church is round, taking the shape of the circular Roman tower upon which it was built. This is the country's most significant Coptic place of worship. ⓐ Sharia Mar Girgis ⏱ 08.30–16.00 Ⓜ Metro: Mar Girgis

Al-Muallaqah (Hanging Church)

This, the oldest and most famous church in Egypt, is believed to have been constructed in the fourth century. Entering the grounds, you will walk through a beautiful courtyard that includes several colourful mosaics depicting different episodes from Jesus' life.

The church itself is glorious, built in warm woods and decorated with red hues. The nave is situated above a Roman gate, which earned the structure its name, the Hanging Church. ⓐ Sharia Mar Girgis 🕐 09.00–16.00 (except during services) Ⓜ Metro: Mar Girgis

Nilometer

This is located on the breezy, southern tip of Rhoda Island, beside the Monastirli Palace. Nilometers were used in Pharaonic times to measure flood levels, but this one dates to the Umayyad period, when Amr Ibn al-As was first settling in Egypt. The structure is one of the oldest in Cairo. ⓐ Sharia al-Malek as-Saleh, Rhoda Island

Pharaonic Village

A trip to this village is a fun way to introduce children to Egypt's ancient history. Families ride in a boat down the Nile with actors reproducing the life of the ancient Egyptians. Children will enjoy watching how papyrus was made and will have great fun with the souvenirs in the gift shop. Incidentally, if you want to buy papyrus, this is a good place to find high-quality examples.
ⓐ 3 Sharia el-Bahr el-Aazam, Giza 📞 (03) 571 8675 or 571 8676 Ⓦ www.pharaonicvillage.com 🕐 09.00–18.00 (often until 21.00 in summer) Ⓜ Metro: Midan Giza, then taxi to Pharaonic Village

Saqqara Pyramids

The captivating Saqqara Pyramids are often overlooked by visitors, which makes a trip here a more tranquil and somehow adventurous experience than one to their Giza counterparts. Located 16 km (10 miles) south of the Sphinx, they were once the most important necropolis of Memphis. The Step Pyramid of Pharaoh Djoser is a colossal monument that was begun around 2630 BC, which makes it the world's first pyramid. Here you will find the original burial site of the kings of the first two dynasties, as well as other early tombs dating from the first three dynasties. ● 08.00–16.00 Oct–Apr; 08.00–17.00 May–Sept (15.00 during Ramadan) ❶ Make sure your taxi driver waits for you as there is no other transport. Admission charge

CULTURE

Coptic Museum
A stop at this museum will give you a peek into the history of Christianity in Egypt. Housed in a Babylonian fort built

▲ Ancient artifacts in the Coptic Museum

by the Romans, its collections include frescoes, ivory, pottery, paintings and other special items that vividly tell the story of the country's Copts. ⓐ Sharia Mar Girgis, Coptic Cairo ⓣ (02) 362 8766 ⓛ 09.00–17.00 Ⓜ Metro: Mar Girgis. Admission charge

Monastirli Palace & Umm Kolthum Museum

On the southern tip of Rhoda Island lies a palace surrounded by a beautiful garden. This is the former residence of the influential Monastirli family. Part of the palace is now used for cultural events, while the other part is home to a museum dedicated to the late Egyptian singing legend, Umm Khulthum. The museum includes the diva's personal items, which range from the notebooks in which

ⓞ *The Solar Barque*

she practised her French to handbags, clothing and the signature sunglasses that she wore at so many of her memorable performances. A short film will introduce you to the darling of the Arab musical world, whose voice still seems to echo down Cairo's streets. ⓐ Sharia al-Malek as-Saleh, Rhoda Island ⓣ (02) 363 1467 ⓛ 09.00–16.00. Admission charge

Solar Barque Museum

Located on the south side of the Great Pyramid, this museum is a superb showcase for the excavated and reconstructed 'solar boat', the world's oldest vessel. The 'Barque' was buried along with the Pharaoh for use on his supposed 'daily journey with the sun across the sky' and was discovered close to the Giza Pyramids. ⓐ Giza Plateau ⓛ 09.00–16.00 Oct–May; 09.00–17.00 June–Sept. Admission charge

RETAIL THERAPY

First Residence Mall Some of Cairo's most exclusive shopping, including the creations of international and local high-end designers, can be found here. The concourse is connected to the Four Seasons First Residence hotel. ⓐ First Residence Complex, 35 Sharia al-Giza, Giza ⓛ 10.00–23.00

Maadi Grand Mall Many Maadi residents remain loyal to this old-time shopping centre. Most stores are Egyptian, making this a centre for bargains and a distinctly different shopping experience. ⓐ 250 Koleyet, Midan al-Nasr, Maadi ⓣ (02) 519 5380 ⓛ 11.00–00.00

Souq El Fustat Between the churches of Coptic Cairo and the Mosque of Amr Ibn al-As you will find this wonderful indoor market that sells many a fine handicraft product, including colourful stitch-work from the south of Egypt, clay pots and fine *galabiyas* (loose robes). This recent addition to the city's shopping spectrum is another option for those who would rather avoid haggling. The quality of the products is considerably better than what's on offer in Islamic Cairo; prices are also higher, though. On site there are workshops and a pottery village. ⓐ Corner of Sharia al-Imam & Sharia Hassan al-Anwar, Coptic Cairo ⓛ Daily (hours vary) ⓝ Metro: Mar Girgis

⬥ *Bargain for Egyptian scarves in the souqs*

TAKING A BREAK

Lucille's ££ ❶ The closest thing to a real American diner in the city, Lucille's is probably best known for its breakfast, which is served every day until 23.00 if you fancy a lie-in. In addition to pancakes, biscuits and gravy you can also order the best hamburgers in the city. ⓐ 54 Road 9, Maadi ⓣ (02) 359 2778 ⓛ 08.00–00.00 ⓜ Metro: Maadi

Villa 55 ££ ❷ Located on trendy Road 9, this villa-turned-restaurant has a spacious garden that's just perfect for whiling away the afternoon and evening. There's an extensive menu, including superb desserts and good shisha. ⓐ 55 Road 9, Maadi ⓣ (02) 735 0470 ⓛ 12.00–00.00 ⓜ Metro: Maadi

Hard Rock Café £££ ❸ If a lack of hamburgers and baps is causing withdrawal symptoms, you will find this location a life-saver. It has a particularly impressive view of the Nile. ⓐ Grand Hyatt, off Corniche el-Nil, Rhoda Island ⓣ (02) 532 1277 ⓛ 11.00–05.00

AFTER DARK

Abou Shakra ££ ❹ For excellent grill and traditional Middle-Eastern fare, including rice-stuffed grape leaves and roasted pigeon, Abou Shakra is a popular choice among Egyptian families – recommendation enough. ⓐ 74 Tariq al-Nasr, Maadi ⓣ (02) 703 1333 ⓛ 12.00–01.00 ⓦ www.aboushakra.com ⓜ Metro: Maadi

Bua Khao ££ ❺ This Thai restaurant serves delicious and authentic dishes. A quiet and laid-back atmosphere makes this a great escape from inner-city hassles. ⓐ 151 Road 9, Maadi ☏ (02) 358 0126 🕐 12.00–22.30 Ⓜ Metro: Maadi

Max's ££–£££ ❻ Understated decor, excellent service and first-rate food. Max himself, the restaurant's owner, is often here. ⓐ 17 Road 263, Maadi ☏ (02) 516 3242 🕐 12.00–00.00

Aqua £££ ❼ If you are looking to really treat yourself, head to the Four Seasons' seafood restaurant. A glorious view of the Nile and some of the best fish and seafood in the city. ⓐ Four Seasons Hotel Cairo at Nile Plaza, 1089 Corniche el-Nil, Garden City ☏ (02) 761 6876 🕐 20.00–01.00

Nile Pharaoh Dinner Cruises £££ ❽ If you don't mind joining the other tourists, Nile cruise options are enjoyable affairs, consisting of buffet-style dinners with a belly dancer and musical performances thrown in. The cruise lasts two hours. ⓐ Sharia Gamal Abdel Nasr, Giza, south of Sheratan ☏ (03) 570 1000 🕐 Departures: 14.30, 19.00, 21.45; cruises last 2 hrs

Tabouleh £££ ❾ A Lebanese-style restaurant with a wide range of *mezzehs* on offer as well as some original main dishes. ⓐ 1 Sharia Latin America, close to the American Embassy compound, Garden City ☏ (02) 792 5261 🕐 12.00–02.00 Ⓜ Metro: Sadat

---

▶ *The seafront in Alexandria*

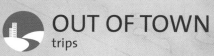

OUT OF TOWN
trips

Alexandria

Only two hours away from the capital is Egypt's Mediterranean gem, Alexandria. Alexander the Great established its timeless importance when he made it his capital, and, as recently as the 19th century, the city was the region's hub of commerce, bringing together a mix of Greeks, Italians, French, Jews and Arabs from the Levant. It was for years a melting pot that reflected cosmopolitan diversity in its every action. However, when Egypt controversially nationalised the Suez Canal, the subsequent attacks by Britain, France and Israel reduced Alexandria to a bleak shadow of its former self. Many foreigners fled, leaving the diminished shell behind them. Happily, all that is now changing.

GETTING THERE

By rail

There are trains for Alexandria departing nearly every hour from Mahattat Ramses (Ramses Station, in Ramses Square). Opt for the Express, which takes approximately two hours (the regular train has several stops and is less comfortable). When you arrive in Alexandria there are two options for disembarking. **Mahattat Misr** (Cairo Station ☎ (03) 392 5985) is the most convenient for Downtown Alexandria destinations, while **Mahattat Sidi Gaber** (Sidi Gaber Station ☎ (03) 426 3953) is best if you're staying in the eastern suburbs.

⬤ *Bibliotheca Alexandrina by night*

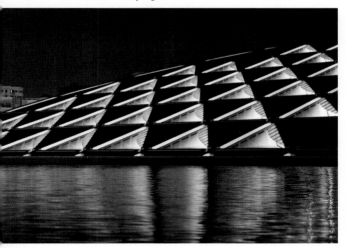

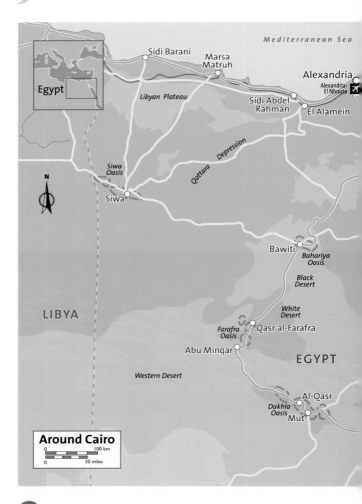

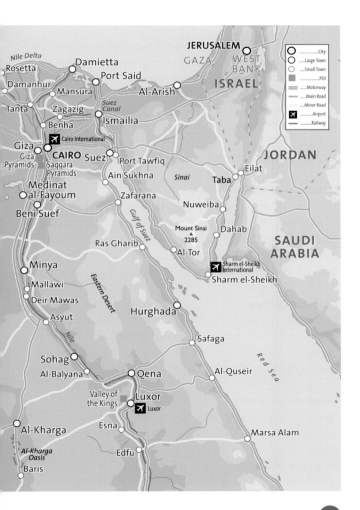

JERUSALEM
GAZA WEST BANK
ISRAEL

Nile Delta
Rosetta
Damietta
Port Said
Al-Arish
Damanhur
Mansura
Tanta
Zagazig
Suez Canal
Benha
Ismailia
JORDAN
Giza
Cairo International
Giza Pyramids
CAIRO
Suez
Port Tawfiq
Saqqara Pyramids
Ain Sukhna
Eilat
Medinat al-Fayoum
Zafarana
Sinai
Taba
Beni Suef
Nuweiba
Ras Gharib
Mount Sinai 2285
Dahab
SAUDI ARABIA
Al-Tor
Minya
Eastern Desert
Sharm el-Sheikh International
Mallawi
Sharm el-Sheikh
Deir Mawas
Asyut
Hurghada
Nile
Safaga
Sohag
Red Sea
Al-Balyana
Qena
Al-Quseir
Valley of the Kings
Luxor
Luxor
Al-Kharga
Esna
Marsa Alam
Al-Kharga Oasis
Edfu
Baris

Legend:
City
Large Town
Small Town
POI
Motorway
Main Road
Minor Road
Airport
Railway

Gulf of Suez

105

By road

From Cairo, Alexandria is a simple trip by road. If you don't have a car, it's around three hours by bus. You can choose between Superjet and West Delta, departing from Turgoman or Al Mazza. The Superjet leaves every 30 minutes from 05.30 to 22.00, while West Delta runs buses between 05.00 and 02.00; both cost around 25LE for a single adult ticket.

SIGHTS & ATTRACTIONS

Catacombs of Kom Al-Shoqafa

The largest Roman burial site in Egypt, the catacombs include a funeral banquet hall and a combination of Pharaonic and Greek flourishes. A visit to this haunting location makes for a shady break in the middle of a hot day. ⓐ Carmous ⓣ (03) 484 5800 ⓛ 09.00–17.00. Admission charge

Citadel of Qaitbay

Built on the ruins of the Lighthouse of Alexandria as a defensive fortress in the 15th century, the citadel perches on the sea coast like a giant sandcastle. ⓐ Eastern Harbour ⓣ (03) 486 5106 ⓛ 09.00–15.00, 16.00–20.00. Admission charge

Roman Amphitheatre

This second-century amphitheatre is a large marble auditorium that rivals any Roman site in the world. ⓐ Sharia Yousef, off Midan Gumhiriyya ⓣ (03) 486 5106 ⓛ 09.00–17.00. Admission charge

CULTURE

Alexandria Contemporary Arts Forum

A non-profit exhibition space showcasing emerging Egyptian and international artists. ⓐ 10 Sharia Hussein Hassab, Azarita ⓣ (03) 480 4145 ⓦ www.acafspace.org

🔺 *Qaitbay fort*

Alexandria Opera House

The beautifully refurbished space, formerly the Sayyid Darwish Theatre, hosts many of the city's opera and classical musical performances. ⓐ 22 Tariq al-Horreya ⓣ (03) 486 5106

ALEXANDRIA'S REVIVAL

The last decade has seen remarkable revitalisation of the city, with several projects restoring Alexandria to its previous splendour. The Bibliotheca Alexandrina (see page 111) shines on a renovated Corniche that includes a broadened promenade, underpasses to cross the busy street and the beautiful Stanley Bridge. Another sign of the city's resurgence is the Four Seasons Hotel Alexandria (see page 115), complete with a luxury shopping centre in its concourse. With new restaurants and cafés springing up, the city is riding on a wave of optimism. Plus, there are plans to restore the Eastern Harbour with an underwater archaeology museum, a waterfront promenade and several hotels, including one inspired by the Pharaohs' lighthouse, whose ruins lie underwater.

Alexandria has never stopped being a favourite destination for Egyptians, who love to lounge on a beach under the Mediterranean sun and enjoy the day's fresh catch at sunset in one of the city's many fine seafood restaurants. An Alexandrian evening can start with a show, be followed by a walk along the Corniche and culminate in a late-night nibble against a backdrop of the sea.

● *The Catacombs of Kom Al-Shoqafa*

Bibliotheca Alexandrina

Since its 2004 opening, the library has become the intellectual and cultural hub of the city. Built near the site of the original Library of Alexandria, the Bibliotheca revives the memory of its predecessor with incredible resources, including shelf space for eight million books. You can browse the antiques museum and rare manuscript galleries, as well as view one of the rotating exhibitions. ⓐ Sharia Shatby ⓣ (03) 483 9999 ⓦ www.bibalex.org ⓛ 11.00–17.00 Sun, Mon, Wed & Thur, 15.00–19.00 Fri & Sat. Admission charge

RETAIL THERAPY

Attarine An antiques shop district filled with cluttered establishments selling dusty European furniture and trinkets dating back to Napoleonic times. You will also find on display the belongings of the many foreigners who fled the country in the 1952 revolution. Even if you don't intend to buy any of the items on sale, it's great fun to browse – almost like being in an historical museum. ⓛ 12.00–21.00

Green Plaza If you are with the kids and looking to relax for an afternoon in the company of local families, this plaza in the suburb of Smouha has a playground, a ten-pin bowling alley and a cinema. Most impressive is the extensive range of boutiques and restaurants. ⓐ End of the Kubri 14th of May, along the Agricultural Road to Cairo ⓛ 11.00–23.00

◀ *El Montazah Palace Gardens*

San Stefano Mall You will find this shopping centre at the bottom of the Four Seasons complex. Local and international outlets sit alongside coffee shops and restaurants in this popular hangout. ⓐ 399 Sharia el-Geish ⓣ (03) 581 8000 ⓛ 13.00–01.00

Zan'et el-Sittat The name of this shopping quarter translates as 'area crowded with women', and you can well see why. Crammed with shops selling household items, fabrics, scarves and other knick-knacks, it has been buzzing with Alexandrian women for decades. If you are looking for cheap buys and interesting sights, this is your place.

TAKING A BREAK

Café Trianon £ This old-time favourite, famous for its coffee and desserts, is a city landmark on the ground floor of the restored Metropole Hotel. ⓐ 52 Sharia Saad Zaghloul ⓣ (03) 486 0986 ⓛ 07.00–00.00

El Montazah Palace Gardens Although picnicking is not common in Cairo, these beautiful palace gardens are fantastic for a stroll before enjoying a coffee and pastry from one of the local cafés.

Qudora ££ A gem for first-class seafood. You will dine on narrow tables on a side street with the city's seasoned seafood fans. Choose fresh fish from packed ice displays. ⓐ 33 Sharia Bairam at-Tonsi ⓣ (03) 480 0405 ⓛ 09.00–15.00

● *The classical Café Trianon*

AFTER DARK

Alexandria's seafood is some of the best in the world. Fish is typically fried or grilled and served with plates of shrimps. In many restaurants you can pick out the exact fish you want and it is prepared to your requirements while you take the edge off your appetite via dishes of salads and spreads.

Fish Market ££ A favourite of Alexandrian and Cairene tourists alike, this is the place for fresh fish selections and a view of the Eastern Bay. ⓐ Corniche, beside Kashafa ⓣ (03) 480 5114 ⓛ 12.30–01.30

The Greek Club ££ Opposite the Citadel, the Greek Club offers wonderfully fresh fish with a side dish of marvellous sea views. ⓐ Sharia Qasr Qaytbay ⓣ (03) 480 1706

Sea Gull Restaurant £££ This old castle used to be Napoleon Bonaparte's home. Now a family restaurant, it is a bit of a trek out of town but the seafood is worth the trip. Consider a late lunch here and stay for sunset. ⓐ Al-Agami Road, near the Desert Road to Cairo ⓣ (03) 440 8777 ⓦ www.seagullegypt.com

ACCOMMODATION

Hotel Crillon £ A well-known budget hotel, this is a clean and reputable place to rest your head. Some rooms have balcony seafront views, while others have en suite bathrooms. ⓐ 5 Sharia Adib Ishaq ⓣ (03) 480 0330

The Union Hotel £ This simple, clean hotel with sea views is one of the best budget options in Alexandria. ⓐ 164 Sharia 26th of July ⓣ (03) 480 7312

The Four Seasons Hotel Alexandria at San Stefano £££ One of the latest additions to the accommodation scene and the most luxurious option in town, this comfortable hotel is in the centre of the Corniche, half-way between Montezza and the harbour. ⓐ 399 el-Geish Road ⓣ (03) 581 8000 ⓦ www.fourseasons.com

El-Salamlek Palace Hotel £££ Situated on a hill overlooking the sea at Montazah Bay, the setting is perfect for a city getaway. Surrounded by gardens, the hotel's interior recreates the glamour of a royal dwelling. ⓐ El Montazah Palace Gardens ⓣ (03) 547 7999

🔺 *The enticing pool and sea views at El-Salamlek Palace Hotel*

The Western Desert Circuit

Discovering Egypt's deserts will introduce you to a variety of stunning landscapes, from rock formations to incredible expanses of red, white or even black sand. If you are willing to travel only four hours from Cairo, you will experience some of the most breathtaking views in the world. You can explore the desert by foot, camel or 4x4. There is a variety of reliable tour companies (see page 118) that will take you from your hotel door to the dunes. If you are not booking a full tour, which is really the best value, you can travel between oases on buses and private-hire minibuses.

Don't be hesitant about leaving the cultural attractions of the city behind: the oases have their own Pharaonic and Roman vestiges. If you're lucky, you may be entertained on your trip by your Bedouin guides, with songs around the campfire and dancing under the stars.

The Western Desert Circuit includes the oases of Bahariya (see page 119) and Dakhla (see page 121). Winding your way through the desert from the former will afford the most fruitful short-haul desert exploration; a longer trip could include the latter. Explorers who are in no rush can include the further-flung oases of Farafra, Al-Kharga and Siwa in their trek, but these require much more time. Shops, eating establishments and clubs barely exist in any organised fashion here. Welcome to another world.

GETTING THERE

By road
While you can access and visit the different oases without a

◒ *The unusual landscape of the White Desert*

special vehicle or licence, trips into the deserts, which are really a must if you have come this far, must be done with special tour operators. There is a wide variety of excellent ones to choose from (see below) and booking is usually very easy and can be made as little as a few days in advance. Of course, if you book earlier, you will be a in a better position to ensure you get the company you want and may even be able to negotiate on the price.

The Upper Egypt Bus Company (a Sharia Misr (03) 847 3610) runs three daily buses between Bawiti, the main town in Bahariya, and Cairo. Buses usually depart at 06.30, 10.00 and 15.00. The trip takes approximately four hours and costs 25LE.

SMOOTH OPERATORS

Heading out into the desert requires a permit for some destinations, not to mention full supplies and experience, so you will want to choose your tour operator carefully. The following are highly recommended companies and trek outfits:

Al-Badawiya An established and highly regarded family operation. In addition to their regular treks, they also offer hiking trips and even jaunts for those looking to work on their Arabic language or belly dance moves in the desert. There's even an annual group expedition for a desert clean-up. (02) 575 8076 www.badawiya.com

Khalifa Expeditions This Bawiti-based group is a reliable

❶ Even if you are travelling in an air-conditioned vehicle, you should still make sure that you apply lashings of sunscreen, wear sunglasses and – most importantly – drink lots of water.

BAHARIYA

Egypt's oasis are the most varied in the world. Some visitors come exclusively for the desert treks, but if you're only on an excursion your best choice is to explore the Bahariya, the closest to Cairo at 365 km (227 miles). With a rich Pharaonic and Roman history, you'll find many a cultural delight while you're here. If you

choice for treks, either by 4x4 or by camel. They host trips for artists who wish to immortalise the landscape on canvas.
❶ (02) 847 3260 or 321 5445 ❷ www.khalifaexp.com

Pan Arab Tours In business for over thirty years, Pan Arab Tours offers a variety of desert experiences with knowledgeable guides and has eco-friendly policies.
❸ 5 El Nozha Street, Heliopolis, Cairo ❶ (02) 418 4409
❷ www.panarabtours.com

Memphis Tours With an extensive variety of desert-trekking packages and several years of experience in the sands, this tour company is a trustworthy option.
❸ 1 Sharia Morad, Midan Giza ❶ (03) 571 6050 or 572 6111
❷ www.memphistours.com

opt to take the bus, you will be greeted on arrival by tour guides
and touts hoping to attract tourists to their hotels and trips.
Tourist Office ❶ (02) 847 3835
Tourist Police ❶ (02) 847 3900

SIGHTS & ATTRACTIONS

Crystal Mountain
In the desert, a short drive away from Bawiti, you will come
across an exquisite deposit of quartz crystal. Do wander the
terrain here and examine crystal pieces, but don't attempt to
take anything away from the site.

Al-Mathaf Museum
Around 200 mummies of men, women and children are the focus
of this museum. This is your chance to get up close and personal
with them. They illustrate a different style of mummification

● *The Dakhla oasis*

DAKHLA

If you want to travel through the desert from Bahariya, you can make your way down to Dakhla. The trip takes four hours. The Upper Egypt Bus Company (see page 118) runs a service from Bahariya to Dakhla that costs 30LE. While most of your sightseeing will probably be done en route, there are still notable things to see in this oasis.

The ancient ruins of Mut el-Kharab can be found just outside the centre of Dakhla. Since the area is believed to have been inhabited from the earliest times of the ancient Egyptians, remnants of a variety of dynasties can be found, although it's thought that most of the old city still remains unexcavated. Dakhla's cultivated land ends at the foot of rock formations, where you will find prehistoric carvings. The once-spectacular depictions of camels, giraffes and other animals are remarkably clear given their age, which leads archaeologists to conclude that they were probably covered by earth until fairly recently. As visitors have explored this site, many have vandalised its walls.

from the ones that can be seen in Cairo's Egyptian Museum.
ⓐ Sharia al-Mathaf ⓣ (03) 847 1633 ⓒ 08.00–14.00

Old Bawiti

For local history outside of museum walls, walk through Bawiti's old quarters. South of the main road you will find the mud brick houses that the desert dwellers have lived in for centuries. Although

● *Exploring the White Desert*

some of the homes are now only abandoned remnants, others are still inhabited.

Palmeries of Bawiti

A great way to enjoy oasis life is to stroll through the palmeries (orchards) of apricots, dates and other fresh produce. They offer majestic shade and will give you a rare glimpse of greenery. The tourist office or your hotel concierge can tell you the best routes to take.

Springs

There are a number of hot and cold springs to choose from in the oases. El-Beshma, or the Roman spring, has a beautiful view, but you probably won't want to swim here. If you go a bit further out, the Bir al-Muftella is best at night because of its hot temperatures. This spring affords a lovely vista of the oasis. In most of the springs, women will feel more comfortable wearing a t-shirt over their swimsuit.

Temple of Alexander

The Temple of Alexander the Great is a sightseeing stop for many tourists. While this is an archaeologically significant find, strong desert winds and a poor restoration project have left the temple rather worn.

ACCOMMODATION

Bawiti has the best selection of accommodation in the Western Desert. You won't find any luxury destinations, but you will find good value. If you do decide to sleep in the oasis instead of the desert, be sure to make your arrangements before you arrive so that you won't be swindled by touts when you arrive. Most places run their own desert treks and can offer exploration tips.

Alpenblick Hotel £ The oldest hotel in the oasis, it has the benefit of a great location. A comfortable stay with a friendly atmosphere. ⓐ Off Sharia Misr ⓣ (02) 482 6150 or 582 3356 ⓦ www.alpenblick-hotel-oasis.com

Desert Safari Home £ This is a friendly hotel with a common garden and kitchen where travellers swap stories of their desert experiences. Climb up to the roof for a peaceful view of an oasis sunrise. The hotel has its own restaurant and bar. ⓣ (03) 847 1321 or 731 3908

BEDOUIN LIFE

Many Bedouin live today as they did thousands of years ago, moving through the desert, using the resources in one area while land replenishes itself naturally in other areas. Traditionally, they have long travelled in small bands and lived in tents, although some now use more secure dwellings. The radical changes that they have experienced in recent years signal a transition from a nomadic to a more modern existence.

El-Beshmo Lodge ££ This long-time favourite is situated beside the El-Beshmo spring. The rooms fall short of spectacular, but the restaurant is a friendly hangout with good food. ⓐ By El-Beshmo spring ⓣ (03) 847 3500 ⓦ www.beshmolodge.com

Minamar Hotel ££ Hotel manager Hendy Taha plays host at this comfortable lodge. Each room has its own bathroom and private balcony overlooking the Bahariya Lake. With extensive facilities from laundry to bike rentals, this small hotel oozes oasis charm. ⓐ Bawiti ⓣ (02) 517 3803 ⓦ www.minamar.com

▶ *Cairo Airport*

PRACTICAL
information

Directory

GETTING THERE
By air

There are lots of easy connections between Cairo and many European cities. If you're starting your trip outside Europe, you will often need to stop over in Europe. The national airline is **EgyptAir** (☎ (02) 267 4700/9 🌐 www.egyptair.com.eg), and while its service levels may not quite be on a par with those of its European competitors, they're really perfectly adequate. You can save money if you purchase your round-trip ticket from Europe (if you do it from Egypt, you'll be hit with hefty taxes).

Just some of the many reliable airlines that have established offices in Cairo are:

Air France ⓐ 2 Midan Talaat Harb, Downtown ☎ (02) 770 6262 🌐 www.airfrance.com

British Airways ⓐ 1 Sharia Abdel Salam Aref, Midan Tahrir, Downtown ☎ (02) 578 9975 🌐 www.britishairways.com

KLM ⓐ 11 Sharia Qasr el-Nil, Downtown ☎ (02) 574 7004 🌐 www.klm.com.eg; additionally Cairo Airport Terminal 1 ☎ (02) 696 1622

Lufthansa ⓐ 6 Midan Sheikh al-Marsafy, Zamalek ☎ (02) 19380 🌐 www.lufthansa.com

Olympic Airlines ⓐ 23 Qasr el-Nil, Downtown ☎ (02) 393 1277 or 393 1318 🌐 www.olympicairlines.com

Many people are aware that air travel emits CO_2, which contributes to climate change. You may be interested in the possibility of lessening the environmental impact of your flight through **Climate Care** (ⓦ www.climatecare.org), which offsets your CO$_2$ by funding environmental projects around the world.

ENTRY FORMALITIES

Ensure that your passport is valid for at least six months after your return flight date and that you are holding a return or onward airline ticket. You will need a visa, which you can purchase either prior to or upon arrival in Egypt. The current fee is $15 or 80LE (about £10) for visas issued at Cairo International airport.

All items of a personal nature are exempt from duty, but electronic equipment, video cameras and laptop computers must be declared and may be listed on a declaration form by a Customs Official, who will retain the original and give you the

◔ Cairo's black and white taxis are one of the easiest ways to get about

copy. Keep this safe with the rest of your travel documents in case you need it when you depart.

MONEY

The Egyptian pound (written 'LE') is the national currency. There are 100 piastres to one Egyptian pound. Paper denominations come in quarter (25 piastres), half (50 piastres) and single pound notes. A few single pound notes will be useful for tipping people who provide such kindnesses as bringing coals for a dying shisha. Five and ten pound notes are useful for taxis. For other items, you will need 20, 50 and 100LE notes. When buying smaller items, many vendors will not be able to provide change for large notes, so try to keep small notes on you at all times. Some touts by the pyramids will ask for US dollars, but you will be fine carrying exclusively local currency.

There are plenty of ATMs in Cairo, mostly in hotels and outside banks, all of which offer service in English. Most have a maximum withdrawal of 4,000LE per day. If you plan to spend more than this, ensure that you have cash to exchange. Currency can be exchanged at banks or conversion offices. The latter can be found around Midan Tahrir, Sharia 26th of July in Zamalek and Mohandiseen.

Visa and Mastercard are accepted at most places, but in some cases there is a minimum purchase amount of 100LE.

HEALTH, SAFETY & CRIME

It's best to drink exclusively bottled water and to avoid ice, which is made with tap water and may be contaminated. Some people recommend avoiding raw fruits and vegetables completely and eating only freshly-cooked vegetables at reputable restaurants. If you do decide to risk fruit, go for bananas and oranges which you can peel yourself. To avoid picking up a gastro-intestinal infection, think carefully about the hygiene of what you eat and drink. If you are in need of medical attention, contact a doctor immediately. You will find that medical services are of a high standard (see page 136). On no account should you consider swimming in the Nile.

For such a large city, Cairo is very safe, and there's little crime. There is a large expatriate community in the city and most Cairenes encounter *el-aganeb* (foreigners) with some regularity. Still, you may encounter some staring, and taxi drivers and restaurant staff may ask you questions about your background. This is almost always friendly, although sometimes people can ask very personal questions. Don't hesitate to demur if you do not wish to answer.

The most common transgression is street harassment of women, which has become an issue for both Egyptian and foreign women. This usually takes the form of catcalls and lewd comments and very rarely extends to prying hands. It's best to look straight ahead and walk confidently. Sunglasses are helpful to avoid eye contact. Downtown tends to be the worst area for this sort of behaviour, although embassy and bank guards in Zamalek and Mohandiseen are also major offenders.

There is no distinct gay community in the city. Homosexual relations should be kept low-key to avoid being apprehended by police. The infamous Queen Boat incident, where a Nile cruise was raided and 52 men were tried and charged for 'offending religion and practising debauchery', has served as a warning. While there is no explicit mention of sexuality in the Egyptian legal code, charges relating to public indecency are sometimes levelled in a fashion that Westerners would regard as homophobic. Gay travellers are advised to exercise discretion. Within Egyptian culture it is the norm for men to hold hands while walking and it is customary for members of the same sex to kiss each other on the cheek when greeting, but overt contact beyond this will gain unwelcome attention and foster potential conflict. Rarely do men and women greet each other with kisses.

OPENING HOURS

Cairo is truly a city that never sleeps. Restaurants will never usher their patrons out to close shop and usually stay open until 01.00 or 02.00. Generally, banks and government services are open between 09.00 and 14.00. Shopping centres open between 11.00 and 00.00, while street boutiques keep their own hours, usually between 10.00 and 22.00. Don't be surprised if opening hours vary from store to store or from day to day and work on an ad hoc basis. Schedules and timings are more fluid in Cairo, so you will have to surrender to the wills of shopkeepers and store clerks.

TOILETS

Automated public toilets for both men and women exist in some places in Downtown. A small fee allows you into the metallic cylinder. Most Egyptians rely on a bidet, so be sure to carry your own tissues or toilet paper if you don't want to go native. In many facilities you will encounter a woman who is responsible for the premises. She may or may not have the tissues you require. Either way, a 2LE tip is the custom. Try your best to heed nature's summons while you're in your hotel or a restaurant to save yourself an unwanted adventure.

CHILDREN

Cairo is a child-friendly city, and indeed you will probably gain attention from locals who will want to play with or hold your children. No Egyptian will ever suggest that you leave your child at home, but you may want to check to confirm that a Nile cruise dinner or evening show for tourists has a child-friendly policy. Sometimes children have difficulty adjusting to Cairo's temperatures, and they should be careful of drinking fresh juices and eating vegetables. Experiences that children often enjoy include the Pharaonic Village (see page 94) and Fagnoon (see page 89), as well as felucca or carriage rides. Al-Azhar Park (see page 32) has a mini-train that takes families on a ride through the grounds. In addition to the gardens, there is also a playground here.

COMMUNICATIONS

Internet

Internet cafés are easy to find anywhere in the Downtown, Zamalek or Mohandiseen neighbourhoods and wireless internet is easy to pick up. All of the American-style coffee shops have access to Wi-Fi, although it is not always free.

Business centres at most hotels will offer internet, but you will be expected to pay up to 50LE per hour instead of the 10LE they ask for in most internet cafés.

Phone

Almost everyone in Cairo owns a mobile phone. Green payphones can be found, but are rarely used. With the loud sounds of the street, making a telephone call from one of these telephones is

TELEPHONING EGYPT

To call Egypt from abroad, dial the international access code (oo from the UK, o11 from the US), followed by Egypt's country code (20), followed by the area code minus the initial zero (2 or 3 for Cairo), followed by the seven-digit number.

TELEPHONING ABROAD

To make an international call from Egypt, dial oo followed by the relevant country code, the area code (usually minus the initial zero), and the local number. Some useful country codes are: Australia 61; Canada 1; New Zealand 64; Republic of Ireland 353; South Africa 27; UK 44; USA 1. For an international operator, dial ☎ 120.

a challenge. Mobiles run on the GSM system and cards can be purchased at street kiosks for compatible phones. There will be an additional fee on the top-up card amount, ranging from 5 to 20LE depending on the amount purchased. To avoid any troubles trying to top up using Arabic instructions, have the shopkeeper add the value to your phone for you. He'll be more than happy to oblige and will probably take the opportunity to strike up conversation.

Post

The national **Egypt Post** service (ⓦ www.egyptpost.org) can be somewhat unreliable. Your trans-Atlantic postcard may arrive in a week, or it may not arrive at all. Having said that, the service has been steadily improving over the last decade. While the postal service operates in English and Arabic, bear in mind that English will not be the first language of the postmaster and print your address very carefully. Post is regularly opened and gifts therein sampled, so be careful with what you decide to post.

You will find green post boxes on the streets. Major hotels will have post offices where you can buy stamps and send your letters. Letters typically take three to five days to Europe, or five to seven days to North America. To guarantee your letter, send it by registered post. For speedy overseas services, use Express Mail Service (EMS). It is more expensive than overseas mail but much less expensive than couriers. Post offices are open between 08.30 and 20.00.

ELECTRICITY

All electrical appliances in Egypt run on 220 volts and the outlets are designed for a two-pin cylindrical plug. Travellers from the UK and US will require plug adaptors, easily obtainable at the airport or an electrical shop in the city. You may also be able to borrow one from the hotel reception.

TRAVELLERS WITH DISABILITIES

High kerbs and choppy pavements make Cairo streets difficult if you have severe physical disabilities. Western hotels, as well as older Egyptian luxury hotels, are equipped with ramps and other facilities for disabled travellers. The good news is that Egypt's influential tourist industry has persuaded many tour operators to make their own arrangements for accessible tours. Check out **Misr Travel** (ⓐ 1 Sharia Talaat Harb ⓣ (02) 393 0010 ⓦ www.misrtravel.net) and Memphis Tours (see page 119) for further information. If you will be arranging your own trip, it is probably best to avoid any of the side streets in Islamic Cairo, while Old Cairo is much friendlier with its smooth lanes, as is the Citadel with its useful ramps.

TOURIST INFORMATION
Ministry of Tourism Headquarters ⓐ Misr Travel Tower, Abbassiyya Square ⓣ (02) 682 8435 or 684 1107 ⓦ www.egypt.travel

Branches of the tourist information office can be found at:

ⓐ Sharia Adly, Downtown ⓣ (02) 390 3000 ⓛ 24 hrs

ⓐ Giza Pyramids ⓣ (03) 385 0259 ⓛ 24 hrs

ⓐ Cairo International Airport ⓣ (02) 418 3132 ⓛ 24 hrs

ⓐ Ramses Railway Station ⓣ (02) 276 4214 ⓛ 24 hrs

BACKGROUND READING

Memories of a Lost Egypt: A Memoir with Recipes by Colette Rossant. A food-related account of a childhood in pre-World War II Cairo.

Cairo: The City Victorious by Max Rodenback. A first-person travelogue that bounces between time periods.

The Cairo Trilogy by Nobel Prize winner Naguib Mahfouz. Includes the memorable *Palace Walk*, *Palace of Desire* and *Sugar Street* and paints a vivid picture of Egyptian life over the last century.

The Prophet Muhammad by Karen Armstrong. A stunning biography that clears up misconceptions and explains the faith that is central to so many Egyptians.

🔽 *Camel-mounted Tourist Police keep a watchful eye at the Pyramids*

Emergencies

The following are emergency free-call numbers:

Ambulance ☎ 123
Emergency road service ☎ (02) 111 0000
Fire ☎ 180
Police ☎ 122
Tourist Police ☎ 126

MEDICAL SERVICES

There are several high-quality hospitals and clinics to choose from. Most doctors speak English, and the following listing is a selection of facilities that are accustomed to treating foreign clients:

Dentists

Dr Muhammad A Farag @ 7 El-Batal Ahmed 'Abd al-'Aziz, Downtown ☎ (02) 393 9161
Dr Raouf Abbassy @ 9 El-Gabalaya, Tonsi Building, Zamalek
☎ (02) 735 1133 or 735 1144

Hospitals

Anglo-American Hospital @ Zamalek ☎ (02) 735 6162/3/4/5
Misr International Hospital @ Doqqi ☎ (03) 760 8261 or 335 3658
As-Salam International Hospital @ Corniche el-Nil, Mohandiseen
☎ (02) 524 0077

POLICE

As a visitor, the best people to turn to for official help if you're the victim of foul play are the Tourist Police.

EMERGENCY PHRASES

Fire!   **Police!**
Harii-a   *Shurta/buliis!*

Can you help me?
Ilha'uuni! (emergency) or Saa'idni? (less urgent)

Call an ambulance/a doctor/the police!
'Ayz/a esa'f /doctoor/shurta!

Tourist Police ⓐ First floor of the building in the alley just left of the Tourist Office Headquarters in Abbassiyya Square ⓣ (02) 620 4508 (in emergency ⓣ 126)

EMBASSIES & CONSULATES
Australia ⓐ World Trade Centre, 1191 Corniche el-Nil ⓣ (02) 575 0444 ⓦ www.egypt.embassy.gov.au
Canada ⓐ 26 Sharia Kamal el-Shenwany, Garden City ⓣ (02) 791 8700 ⓦ www.egypt.gc.ca
New Zealand ⓐ North Tower, Nile City building, Corniche el-Nil, Bulaq ⓣ (02) 461 6000 ⓦ www.nzembassy.com
UK ⓐ 7 Sharia Ahmed Ragheb, Garden City ⓣ (02) 794 0852 ⓦ http://ukinegypt.fco.gov.uk
USA ⓐ 8 Sharia Kamal el-Din Salah, Garden City ⓣ (02) 797 3300 ⓦ http://cairo.usembassy.gov

INDEX

Editorial/project management: Lisa Plumridge
Copy editor: Monica Guy
Layout/DTP: Alison Rayner

The publishers would like to thank the Egyptian Tourist Authority (ETA) and the following individuals and organisations for supplying their copyright photos for this book: Barni/Bauer, page 10; Gary Denham, page 127; David Dennis, page 19; Dreamstime.com (Camhi Franck, pages 84–5; David Garry, page 92); Hyatt Hotels & Resorts, pages 26 & 38; Paul Kist, page 35; Adrian Lindley/123RF, page 55; Nermeen Mouftah, page 13; Mira Pavlakovic/SXC.hu, page 5 Alison Rayner, pages 134–5; Mike Rosenberg, page 66; Amanda Rynes/SXC.hu, page 43; Vyacheslav Stepanyuchenko, page 120; ETA/Bertrand Rieger/ hemis.fr, pages 117 & 122; ETA/Bertrand Gardel/hemis.fr, all others.

Send your thoughts to
books@thomascook.com

- **Found a great bar, club, shop or must-see sight that we don't feature?**
- **Like to tip us off about any information that needs a little updating?**
- **Want to tell us what you love about this handy little guidebook and more importantly how we can make it even handier?**

Then here's your chance to tell all! Send us ideas, discoveries and recommendations today and then look out for your valuable input in the next edition of this title.

Email the above address (stating the title) or write to: pocket guides Series Editor, Thomas Cook Publishing, PO Box 227, Coningsby Road, Peterborough PE3 8SB, UK.

WHAT'S IN YOUR GUIDEBOOK?

Independent authors Impartial up-to-date information from our travel experts who meticulously source local knowledge.

Experience Thomas Cook's 165 years in the travel industry and guidebook publishing enriches every word with expertise you can trust.

Travel know-how Thomas Cook has thousands of staff working around the globe, all living and breathing travel.

Editors Travel-publishing professionals, pulling everything together to craft a perfect blend of words, pictures, maps and design.

You, the traveller We deliver a practical, no-nonsense approach to information, geared to how you really use it.

Useful phrases

Egypt's official language is Arabic, though English is fairly widely spoken. In the phrases below, an apostrophe (') indicates a throaty 'a' produced at the back of the throat, while a speech mark (") indicates a guttural stop. Where two options are given, the first is masculine and the second is feminine.

English	Approx pronunciation
BASICS	
Yes	Na'am
No	La"
Please	Lau samaht/samahti; min fadlak/fadlik
Thank you	Shukran
Hello	Ahlan/ahlan wa sahlan
Goodbye	Aalaamu 'aleekum; ma'a-s-salamaama; salaam
Excuse me, pardon	Baad iznak/nik
I'm sorry	Ana aasif/asfa
That's okay	Kwayis
I don't speak Arabic	Mabakkallimsh 'arabi
Do you speak English?	Tikalamy inglizee?
Good morning	Sabah al-kheir
Good afternoon/evening	Masa" al-khayr
Goodnight	Tisbah ahla khayr
My name is ...	Ismi ...
NUMBERS	
One	Wahid
Two	Itnain
Three	Talaata
Four	Arba'a
Five	Khamsa
Six	Sitta
Seven	Seba'a
Eight	Tamanya
Nine	Tisa'a
Ten	'Ashara
Twenty	'Ashreen
Fifty	Khamseen
One hundred	Maya
SIGNS & NOTICES	
Airport	Al-mattar
Railway Station	Mahattat al-"tr
Platform	Raseef
Smoking/No Smoking	Tadkheen/mamnuya tedkheen
Toilets	Hammaam
Ladies/Gentlemen	A-sittat/a-rigal
Metro/bus	Mehtro/Autobeez